Your L♥ve Numbers™

Discovering the Secrets of Your Life, Loves, & Relationships

Richard Andrew King

Richard King Publications

© by Richard Andrew King
Published by Richard King Publications
PO Box 3621
Laguna Hills, CA 92654

No part of this publication may be reproduced or transmitted in any form or by any means, electronic or mechanical, including photocopy, recording or any information storage and retrieval system now known or to be invented without permission in writing from the publisher, except by a reviewer who wishes to quote brief passages in connection with a review written for inclusion in a magazine, newspaper, online article or broadcast. Contact Richard King Publications, PO Box 3621, Laguna Hills, CA 92654.

This book and its information contains copyrighted material, trademarks, and other proprietary information. You may not modify, publish, transmit, participate in the transfer or sale of, create derivative works of, or in any way exploit, in whole or in part, any Proprietary or other Material including the formulae included herein relating to relationships in any capacity.

Library of Congress Cataloging-in-Publication Data

King, Richard Andrew
Your Love Numbers
ISBN: 978-0-931872-13-6
Date of Publication: 22 February 2011

Formerly published as The 5 Minute Lover
Date of Publication: 12 October 2009

DEDICATION

To everyone who truly wants to love.

www.YourLoveNumbers.com

Acknowledgments

A personal thank you to every person
who has shared their life and numbers,
opening the door to greater
knowledge and understanding of
life, love, and relationships.

A special thanks to Tashia R. Peterman,
graphic artist and photographer,
for her wonderful cover art.
(www.tashiasphotography.com)

Richard Andrew King
PO Box 3621
Laguna Hills, CA 92654-3621
www.richardking.net

Your L♥ve Numbers™

Discovering the Secrets of Your
Life, Loves, & Relationships

Table of Contents

Chapter	Title	Page
	Author's Introduction	9
1	Love and Light	13
2	The Lifepath [LP-Birth Date]	25
3	The Expression [Exp - Birth Name]	71
4	The Performance [PE - Role in Life]	113
5	The Soul [Desires/Needs/Wants]	155
6	The Nature [Personality]	179
7	The Loveline	205
8	The Love Match	223
9	The Love Mix	241
10	Love Bumps	251
11	Love Voids	263
12	Love Notes	285

AUTHOR'S INTRODUCTION

I have been passionately studying numerology since 1980, completely fascinated and magnetized to the relationship between one's numbers and one's life. There is, indisputably, a divine connection between our natal data [full birth names and birth date] and our life. What power exists that is so vastly intelligent it can create destinies for each of us, as well as integrate those destinies with everyone we interact with in life for our entire life, is far beyond my limited capacity to understand. Yet, my experience and research have taught me it is so. Personally, this power is God. Regardless of what label we give such a power, the fact remains that we all have a destiny and a blueprint of our lives that can be read once we understand the keys and codes to unlock their secrets. Unbelievable? Perhaps. True? Bank on it.

My journey into the mysteries of numbers began with a quest to discover why some relationships were great, others good, some not; others horrible. That thirty year search, enormously fruitful and revealing, is the basis of this book which will illustrate, through *The King's Numerology*tm system, how to determine the secrets of your life, loves and relationships in a matter of minutes.

For example, do you truly know what motivates and drives you, your spouse, children, partner, friends? What do they want out of life? Can you help make them happy? Can they help make you happy? Can the two of you find harmony, fulfillment, love and peace in life? What are your assets and liabilities? Those of your family, friends and partners? Will there be attraction between you and another person? Will you be attracted to them but them not to you? Will they be attracted to you but you not attracted to them? Will there be love between the two of you or something else? In effect, what are the keys and codes to finding love?

This book will show you the secret formulas to determine all this and much more. This research is unique, and doesn't exist anywhere else. Although results cannot be guaranteed because there are no guarantees in life, the research findings contained in this work have proven themselves to be quite accurate, and it would be inappropriate for this information not to be shared with others. As the esteemed Dr. Albert Einstein noted: *...The right to search for truth and to publish and teach what one holds to be true... implies also a duty; one must not conceal any part of what one has recognized to be true.*

Frankly, there are far too many unhappy, unfulfilling and short-lived relationships in today's world, not to mention the skyrocketing number of divorces which have such a negative impact upon people's lives, especially the lives of children. The information in this book offers powerful and unique knowledge which can definitely assist people in building strong and meaningful relationships and in finding a person who is truly compatible as a life partner. The method of discovering how to generate excellent relationships which this book teaches may be unorthodox but that's only because it is new. One day, the hope is it will be commonplace, and the reality of broken and unhappy relationships will be more the exception than the rule.

Journeys are often initiated by a seminal event, some catalyst that fires the engines of action. Although I had been studying numerology for decades and discovering many relationship secrets based solely on numbers, I had not felt any definitive impetus to share such truths with the world until it happened. "It" was a situation in which a delightful family had been in emotional distress for nearly two decades because of a simple lack of understanding numbers and their relationship to life. The son's desires were marked by the number Seven (7), the most internal and private of all energies, reflecting an intrinsic need to be private and solitary. The mother's life featured the number (8), the most external and social of all energies. Seven and Eight are opposites. Although the mother was loving, as her son grew she kept encouraging him to be more social and talkative, a life style she embraced but which was directly opposed to his deepest desires, causing him extreme stress. The pain between the mother and son because of this clashing of their life's numbers was obvious and unfortunate. When the numeric reality of their lives was revealed, a light bulb went off. The mother realized the errors in her method of raising her son. She changed. The son's face lit up like a flash of light at midnight. He was finally understood. Peace at last. Yet, it was a painful decades long situation that could have been avoided if the numbers associated with each person's life had been known. After this event, I could wait no more. The discomfort for me was painful but catalyzing. In that moment I felt an inexorable compulsion and duty to share the truths I've learned in hopes that such knowledge will help others lead more loving, harmonious and fulfilling lives.

With warm regards,

Richard Andrew King

Your Love Numbers   King

Chapter One

LOVE & LIGHT

Love and Light. What do they have in common? They are the basis of life. Without light, life as we know it could not exist. Without love, life as we know it would be intolerable. We all need light to survive, and we all need love to survive. A loveless, lightless life is no life at all.

There is another major similarity between love and light. They can both be reduced to numbers. Strange isn't it? But it's true. Remember Pythagoras? He was the famous mathematician, scientist and philosopher who lived approximately 2500 hundred years ago (500 years BCE, before the Common/Christian Era). Aside from being credited with the discovery of the Pythagorean Theorem relating to the hypotenuse of a right triangle, which we learned in geometry class ($a^2 + b^2 = c^2$), he made this astute observation:

> *Numbers rule the universe. Everything is arranged according to number and mathematical shape.*

This is a powerful statement, but how can this be so, that numbers rule the universe? Answer: because everything can be translated and/or reduced into some form of numerical design. Take computers for example. They are totally based in numbers, basically 0s and 1s. In fact, all science, commerce, banking, colors, music, light and sound have numbers at their core. Light, which is basically electromagnetic radiation, can be measured using numbers. Sound, which is simply mechanical vibration, can also be measured using numbers. Interestingly, and quite profoundly, love and attraction between people can also be measured and described using numbers! The purpose of this book is to reveal the numeric keys and codes of love and attraction so you can apply their truth to your life and thereby increase your own personal happiness and fulfillment.

Both light and love are energy. As human beings, each of us and our destinies are energy too, and that energy can be translated into numbers, just like light and sound. When we learn the simple process of reading our own set of personal numbers, as well as those numbers of the people we love or with whom we are associated, we can create a readable numerical configuration, format, structure or outline of love, a *loveline* so to speak. Once learned, the process of knowing someone via their numbers can be done in as little as a few minutes!

When the numbers (energies) between people mix extremely well in their combined or mixed *loveline*, there is the wonderful feeling of attraction, harmony, joy and love. When the numbers between people are discordant and clash, there is detraction, repulsion, discord and little to no love. Therefore, in finding love the key is to find someone whose personal numbers blend extremely well with our own. To reiterate this reality, when the numbers between two people are highly concordant and complementary, there is attraction and love. When the numbers between two people are highly discordant and non-complementary, there is little to no attraction or love. It's as simple as that.

So what are these numbers in our personal *loveline*, how do we find them and what are the secrets to creating an harmonious and fulfilling match using them? That's what this book will address and teach. The process is not hard. In fact, it's very easy, so just because we're going to use numbers, don't panic if you're not number savvy. You don't have to be. All you have to do is be able to add a few numbers together and associate those numbers with their attributes and characteristics, which we'll explain in due time and which a grade school student can understand. This is not only very simple, it's also easy and fun and, most importantly, can help you know who the best spouse, friends and associates will be in your life. When relationships are based on our personal numbers - the intrinsic labels of our personal energy fields, we and those whom we love, will enjoy much more fulfilling and meaningful relationships. Our lives will then be joyful, happy and beautiful.

Benefits

Before we begin learning the numerical design of the loveline, let's discuss the benefits of using numbers as one aspect of generating good relationships. As a pre-note, this process is based on *The King's Numerology* system which has been developed over decades of study, research and application in the realm of relationships. It is real and it works. It may be unconventional and on the fringe of accepted thought but that is because it is unconventional and on the edge of what is considered normal, at least for the time being. It is also because using numbers as a method of assessing relationships is a new idea. Yet, once the process has been studied, applied and proven, its acceptance will become universal and the whole experience of love between people will no longer be a mystery, but a commonly known and actualized reality.

1. Self-Awareness

In establishing our own numeric profile or *Basic Matrix* (*The King's Book of Numerology, Volume I: Foundations & Fundamentals*), we will begin to know ourselves, our needs, wants, desires, personality, purpose, strengths, weaknesses, challenges and path in life. In effect, we will adhere to the ancient Greek admonition, "Know Thyself." If we don't know who we are and what we want, how can we be happy? Each of us does have a God-given right to be happy and fulfilled. If our cup is empty, how can it overflow to help fill someone else's cup? It can't. Therefore, it is not meant that individually we should totally sacrifice ourselves for someone else at the expense of our own well-being. Each of us has a right to our own life. After all, our lives are indeed that, our lives, and we are responsible for them. No one is responsible for us but us. Therefore, to be happy we must do for us to a degree, not to a point of self-absorption and self-centeredness, but to a point of health and wholeness. Think of a new seedling. If it gave away to other seedlings the nutrients in the soil it needed to grow, how could it grow, let alone flourish and create more seed and fruit that could be subsequently shared with others? The fact is, it couldn't. It would die, and dying with it in the process would be a future of potential abundance for all to share. Tragic.

2. Knowing the Other Person

If we're involved in a relationship - whether it is romantic, domestic, social or business-oriented, and we only know or care about who we are and what we want and have no concern for who the other person is, what their needs, wants and desires are, what good is that? It is no good at all. The key to successful relationships is not only knowing what we need but equally knowing what the other person needs and then having each of the partners surrender themselves to the relationship, which is a living entity in itself.

The Relationship

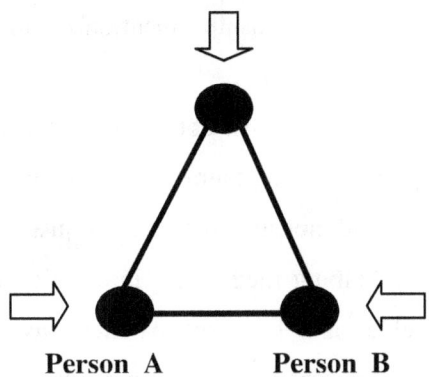

Person A   Person B

It's obvious that if either or both of the individuals are too consumed with themselves and their own needs, wants and desires to the exclusion of the relationship, the triangle will be broken and the relationship will suffer, if not totally collapse. The moral of this little diagram is that all successful relationships in which both or all participants are happy, fulfilled and content are built on a desire to keep the relationship triangle complete. Therefore, each person must be dedicated to making the appropriate sacrifices for the health of the entity that is the relationship, an entity that is built on balance between the partners, i.e., the pillars creating it.

3. Raising of Children

A third benefit is the raising of children. When parents know exactly what their children need, what motivates them, where their lives are taking them and what role they will ultimately give on the great life stage, they can be a wonderful asset in their children's lives. But if they do not truly know nor understand what their children need, regardless of the most loving intent in the world, they may actually be damaging their children. This was illustrated in the mother/son relationship mentioned in the author's introduction.

Raising children is not just about patting them on the back, hugging them, complimenting them, feeding them, clothing them, disciplining them and housing them. It is just as much about guiding them and helping them grow into their own selves and lives, not the selves and lives the parents may want for their children based on their (the parent's) own needs, wants and desires but the children's. Every individual has his own destiny, own personality, character traits, assets, liabilities, strengths and weaknesses and these may be totally incongruent with those of the parents, for good or bad. Yet, how often do parents, in attempting to raise their children, not truly understand what their children need in the deepest sense.

4. Personal Balance

Another major benefit of knowing how numbers work in people's lives is that we learn to honor who we are and not become consumed and imbalanced by attempting to be like someone else, which can never happen anyway. It's fine to emulate the good qualities of another person, but each of us has our own distinct, separate, specific and personal destiny that God gave us. In other words, each of us is uniquely special, a truth that needs to be honored and embraced rather than foregone in lieu of trying to be someone whom we are not. Getting caught up in celebrity worship, as one example, is betraying our own divine blueprint. Why go from cradle to grave consumed with worshiping, idolizing, copying or attempting to be someone else, all the while paying little or no attention to the beautifully divine and unique individual that each of us intrinsically is? By honoring our own life and respecting it rather than ignoring it by worshiping someone else and their life is one method of remaining balanced and content in life. Where there is contentment, there is peace. As Shakespeare poignantly states in *Hamlet*, Act I, Scene iii:

This above all, to thine own self be true and it must follow as the night the day, thou canst not then be false to any man.

5. Sharing the Wisdom

Once we understand by direct experience the truth of numbers as they relate to our lives, we can share such truth with others and by so doing help them understand their lives and increase their happiness and well-being. Once we know, we can never not know. Certainly, knowing is better than not knowing. When we don't know, how can we possibly change or improve our position or relationships? We can't. Yet, when we know, we have power, the power to adjust and work with our destiny and not fight, deprecate or depreciate it in any way but rather be grateful to God that He gave us the opportunity to live, grow, evolve and climb higher on the ladder of life.

Examples

To understand the power of knowing numbers, their relationship to life, and how we can learn from them, let's take a brief look at a few examples of real people, their lives and relationships. The names of the people involved have been changed but the scenarios are all real, taken from The King's Numerology archives.

Example #1: Parent/Child Opposition

This is the example discussed in the introduction. Basically, Jenny was a wonderful, caring and loving mother who had the number 8 [eight] dominate in her numerology chart. Eight [8] is the number of social power and interaction. It is the most external of the basic numbers One [1] through Nine [9] - the *Alpha-Numeric Spectrum* or *Avenue of Crowns*. Her son Jon had the number 7 [seven] dominate in the desire component of his chart. Seven [7] is the most internal of the basic numbers. Seven loves its reclusion, privacy and solitude - all things Jon loved and required for his own well-being.

From the time Jon was born, Jenny encouraged her son to be social because this was her numeric point of reference, although she wasn't versed in numerology and its application to life. As Jon grew, it was obvious he was reclusive. Jenny perceived this to be a problem and kept urging him to be more communicative and social. Tensions grew. Jon's confidence was stifled, his self-image negatively charged.

The problem in this case is that the numbers 7 and 8 are direct opposites. They conflict. Jon's most intimate desires in life were to be reclusive, to be his own best company, to embrace the solitude he loved and needed for his own well-being, to withdraw from social events, not embrace them.

Frankly, there was nothing wrong with Jon at all. Seven energy is not a social energy. Eight is. Had Jenny understood numbers and their relationship to life, the problems and personal esteem issues of her son could have been avoided from birth by having her embrace his need for solitude rather than urging him to be social. This entire experience lasted for sixteen years until Jenny sat in on Jon's numerology reading. It was then she discovered the true needs of her son and her mistake in flooding him with her expectations. After she gained an understanding of her son's needs, she instantly made the corrections, being deeply apologetic to her son for her actions in raising him.

In fairness to Jenny, this parent/child opposition is quite normal. Many teachers are also guilty of the same mistake. There is a belief that being social is normal and that people who are not social are abnormal. Hence, the action of parents and teachers to keep encouraging the children under their care to be social. This is unfortunate and hopefully such misdirected insistence of sociability will change as people become more aware of numbers and how they affect life and destiny. This is not to say that negative anti-social behavior is not problematic, but simply because someone prefers, in fact needs, to be alone is not in and of itself a problem.

Here's a quick reference note regarding numbers. Social energies are marked by the even numbers 2-4-6-8. The odd numbers 1-3-5-7-9 are generally considered creative numbers.

Social vs. Creative Numbers

Social Numbers	2	4	6	8	
Creative Numbers	1	3	5	7	9

The following number sets represent direct opposites. When these numbers appear in a chart or charts, they can create opposition, conflict, confusion.

Numerical Opposites

1 vs. 2
4 vs. 5
7 vs. 8

One rules the self, male and fire; Two rules others, the female and water. Four governs convention and stability; Five is the energy of non-convention and movement. Seven, as noted, rules all things internal; Eight, all things external.

Example #2: Spontaneity vs. Practicality

Alice and Anthony were girlfriend and boyfriend. Alice had a great deal of 4 energy in her chart while Anthony's chart was rich in 5 energy. As we see from the "Numerical Opposites" exhibit above, the numbers 4 and 5 are opposites. Four [4] is practical, traditional, conventional and deliberate. Its element is earth. Symbols for the 4 would be an anchor, roots, chains, even the Rock of Gibraltar. The number Five [5], whose element is fire, is adventurous, non-traditional, unconventional and spontaneous. Five is the energy of diversity, movement and freedom. Symbols for the 5 include wings, wheels and the amorphous element mercury.

One evening, Anthony suggested to his girlfriend that they drive to a theme park a few hours away, sleep in the car and be ready to hit the fun as soon as the gates to the park opened the next morning. As far as Anthony was concerned, he was just reflecting his spontaneous and adventurous 5 self. Alice, however, didn't see things the same way. For her, traveling a couple hours to a theme park, sleeping in a car, and hitting the rides at the amusement park at the break of dawn was not at all practical or adventurous. Was there a problem here? Yep. Wings and roots are not compatible. The result is that they didn't go on Anthony's little adventure. Ultimately, their relationship dissolved, each moving on to find a partner more compatible with their individual interests and energies.

Example #3: Star vs. Servant

Toni was a musician. His dream was to be a rock star. He had a band and worked at his craft. Yet, his dreams weren't being realized and he was frustrated. Eventually, he realized his dream wasn't going to materialize and he turned his energies to being a music producer rather than a rock star. His numbers clearly indicated this condition. His birth name was a One [1], the energy of the self, the star, the independent person and creator. This 1 energy was motivating him to be a rock star. However, the numbers from his birth date were a Two [2], the energy of support and helping others. The numbers of the birth date create what is called the *Lifepath* which is the major component creating the destiny. Although Toni wanted to be the star, the one who is the center of attention, his Lifepath placed him in a role of service, support and helping others rather than being a rock star in the limelight. Thus, Toni became a music producer.

These are just a few examples of how numbers reveal destiny. Let's now move on and learn more about numbers and the process that will reveal our own special destinies and path to personal love.

Chapter Two

THE LIFEPATH
[The Birthdate]

The *Lifepath*, often referred to as the *Birthpath* in numerology, is derived from the day, month and year of our birth. The Lifepath is fixed and cannot be altered. One analogy of the Lifepath is that it is the script of our lives, the screenplay meant for us to act out in this lifetime. It is not who we are. Rather, it signifies the road we will traverse in life.

The energy patterns established in the Lifepath are unbreakable, making our lives destined. These energy patterns are intransigent and will not be comprised. They are not influenced by us in the least. In fact, they influence us to the nth degree. They compel us to move and act in manners commensurate with the unfoldment of our destiny. They bring people, events and circumstances to us. They magnetize us to every deed our destiny calls for us to experience. The energy patterns of the Lifepath comprise the main vibratory structure of our destiny.

Because life is destined, one argument people often espouse is that they will then simply lay down and let everything come to them. In one sense this is correct. Our destiny always comes to us or, from another perspective, forces us to come to it. Regardless of the point of view taken, the vibratory energy fields of our

Lifepath will move us to manifest our destiny. For example, we may choose to go on a camping trip in the woods. However, if the woods catch on fire, we will have to abandon our plans and move to safety, lest the forest fire consume us in its heat and fury. Similarly, we may choose to have a pleasant swim in the ocean, but the currents of the ocean will determine the pleasantness of our swim, not us. In fact, those currents could, because of their strength and overpowering force, pull us out to sea or drown us entirely, taking our life in the process. Likewise, we may build a fortune in the stock market but lose it all because of financial influences beyond our control. Just as the forces of the forest fire, the ocean's currents and the financial climate compel us to move to their will, so the forces of our Lifepath compel us to move in ways appropriate to the fulfillment of its will and of our destiny.

If we spend just a little time analyzing our lives, we will see that many of the decisions we have made in the past, we were forced to make because of conditions, events, people and circumstances extraneous to us. All of these things that happen to us in our lives come through the vibrations of our Lifepath. When we can learn to accept this reality, we can adjust to our lives, allowing them to run their course without us becoming neurotic, imbalanced, discomforted or stressed out in the day-to-day process of living, which will surely happen if we try to force our will upon the massive vibrational tides of our Lifepath.

Another way of perceiving the Lifepath is to consider the analogy of an automated car wash. In the beginning of the washing process, our vehicle is hooked up to a chain which pulls it along its course until the cleansing activity is completed. Once attached to the chain, the car has no choice but to follow the path intended for it. It's life and its activities, for those few moments, are destined and inescapable. Likewise, when we're born, our soul is hooked up to a physical body and chain of events which pull us along until our life ends at death. Once we are attached to this life through the process of birth, we are hooked up to a series of events beyond our control. These events become our destiny. We may experience them weeping or laughing but, to be sure, we will experience what is in our Lifepath to experience and nothing, save the Grace of God, can alter or change the play.

Additionally, another way of viewing the Lifepath is to see it as an energy world to which we are sent for a specified period of time--specifically, the birth-death cycle of our life. For example, as a simple analogy, let's say there exists a numerological solar system of a sun and nine planets. The sun is the Life-force and each of the planets, each of the worlds, is numbered One through Nine. When we are born, God sends us to one of these nine planets, and for our entire life we are made to experience the effects of its vibration. If we are sent to the planet 'One', our lives will be focused solely in its vibratory field. If sent to the planet 'Two', we will experience the attributes and characteristics it manifests and so forth through the entire spectrum of the nine numbers, the nine vibratory worlds. However, once sent to a particular world, i.e., once born into a specific lifepath vibration, we cannot move to another world. We must live on the world to which we were sent and make the best of it. It may not be the world of our choosing. We may not like it and it may be extremely uncomfortable. On the other hand, we may love it and find it quite fulfilling. The point is, all of this is beyond our control. God decides our destiny from life to life. He sends us to the energy world of His choosing, not ours.

Furthermore, to wish to live on or in someone else's world, to be envious or jealous of them, their life style or experiences, or, on the other side of the coin, to ridicule or deprecate others and their existence on another world because we see them as inferior or less fortunate, is unhealthy and dangerous. We each have our own destiny and no one can change it except God, but this is unlikely since He established it in the first place. The key is that we must learn to understand our Lifepath and its special set of vibrational patterns and be comfortable with it and them for they are beyond our control. This is the crux of the prayer which states: "God, grant me the serenity to accept the things I cannot change, the courage to change the things I can, and the wisdom to know the difference."

One final analogy is that our Lifepath is the 'hand' we were dealt at birth. The cards within our 'hand' are exclusive to us. We may be dealt a hand of great fortune or one of little fortune. For most of us, our 'hand' lies somewhere between the two extremes. The point is, however, we cannot change the 'hand' we were dealt at birth. We must play it. It's destiny. In doing so, like every card player knows, we need to keep a poker face throughout the game. In other words, we need to stay balanced, poised and calm as we play out the 'hand' that is our destiny. Dignity is more important than victory. Winning and losing are simply the conditions of polar extremes to and from which the great cosmic pendulum swings to and fro.

Cards Of Life

These are the cards your life has dealt,
so these are the cards you play.
There's no use weeping over cards
that were not dealt your way.

Life is destined to the breath--
a truth we must accept
if we're to find some peace of mind
and live without regret.

We all are actors on a stage,
but the Director sets our role.
Our life performance is a script--
it's the nature of the show.

Therefore, we mustn't be distressed.
No two hands are just the same.
When all is finally said and done,
in the end, it's just a game.

So play the cards your life has dealt,
but play them strait and true,
and, remember, from the Lord's own hand
<u>your</u> cards were dealt for <u>you</u>!

As a final note, all numbers have a positive and a negative polarity to them. Therefore, no number is totally good or totally bad. Each number is what we make of it. Therefore, no Lifepath is good or bad.

Calculating the Lifepath

The calculation of the Lifepath is extremely simple and literally takes seconds. Simply write down the day, month and year of birth in numeric form, add left to right and reduce to a single digit. Let's take some examples.

1. Birth date: 8 January 1960 [January is the 1st calendar month]

8 January 1960

$8 + 1 + 1 + 9 + 6 + 0 = 25 > 2 + 5 = 7$

The Lifepath is 7

[Note: For example purposes later on, we'll associate this birthdate of 8 January 1960 with a fictitious person, Mary Jane Smith.]

2. Birthdate of 14 August 1985 [August is the 8th calendar month]

14 August 1985

$1 + 4 + 8 + 1 + 9 + 8 + 5 = 36 > 3 + 6 = 9$

The Lifepath is 9

[Note: For example purposes later on, we'll associate this birthdate of 14 August 1985 with a fictitious person, John David Doey.]

Now it's your turn. What's your lifepath? Your spouse? Children? Parents? Partners? Family members? Friends?

Day:_____ + Month:_____ + Year:_____ = Lifepath:_____

Lifepath Descriptions

Now that we've learned how to calculate the Lifepath, let's take a look at what each Lifepath represents. Keep in mind that the Lifepath is not the person. The Lifepath is the script of life, the lessons, both positive and negative, to be learned and experienced from cradle to grave.

<u>The 1 Lifepath</u>

One represents the yang aspect of Nature. A fire sign, it is masculine, assertive, creative. One likes to go first and show the way. Therefore, it can lead, and in the Lifepath position, the person will be learning to do and to lead, not to follow; to create, not subordinate; to stand alone, not hold hands with others or follow another; to act, not react. One is the vibration of self-reliance, not reliance on others. It is also the energy of that which is original and unique.

All of this taken into consideration, the One Lifepath will find the person striking out on his or her own. Situations will occur during the life journey which will compel the individual to take the lead - the lead in relationships, the lead in the home as the matriarch or patriarch, the lead at work, at school, in church, in the community and possibly in the business environment as an entrepreneur, manager or leader. Because the element of the One is fire, it heats things up, takes action, initiates, grabs hold of the standard and, while standing out front, says, directly or indirectly, "Follow me!" Therefore, a person with this lifepath lesson will learn to lead - voluntarily or involuntarily. And, furthermore, when these opportunities present themselves, the One Lifepath individual should take charge and not generally relinquish the lead to someone else unless the other person is a leader too.

The One Lifepath is also one in which a person could create, particularly in the realm of mental and artistic self-expression. Any occupation using the mind, words and communication skills would be important in harmonizing with this lifepath, especially if strengthened by Three and Seven energy elsewhere in the chart, particularly in the Basic Matrix. Three rules words and communication while the Seven represents the mind and spirit.

Because One stands alone, people under this vibration make excellent pioneers and adventurers. One is solitary by nature and generally unencumbered by the need to socialize or survive in groups. Being bold, daring, courageous and adventurous are qualities the One Lifepath person would be wise to engender.

The cautionary yellow flag for the One Lifepath is the possibility of the person involved with its energy of becoming too self-oriented, self-consumed, self-possessed, self-centered and ego-maniacal. Huge egos can be destructive, arrogant, imperious, unyielding, unbending. Fire warms and gives life. But too much fire burns, maims and destroys.

Thus, it is pride that may be a major hurdle and stumbling block for the One Lifepath person to overcome. How many conflicts have been generated, how many wars fought, how many people hurt, how much blood spilt, how many tragic tears have been shed because of the weakness and disease of human pride? And, yet, from a spiritual perspective, what is there in this life to be proud of? It is this negative quality of the One Lifepath that should warrant a close eye.

Finally, when One operates at its zenith, it is the beacon of light illuminating the way for others. From a spiritual perspective, One is union with the divine. For those with a One Lifepath the goal is self-reliance, standing on your own two feet, being counted, having courage, going first, often flying solo, playing the role of the maverick, the lone wolf and illustrating, ultimately, what it means to be at one with <u>the</u> One, i.e., God.

The 2 Lifepath

The Two Lifepath addresses the yin, the female aspect of creation. Whereas the One Lifepath focuses on the male energy [yang] and the self, the Two Lifepath focuses on female energy [yin] others, relationships, support, balance, harmony, rhythm, equilibrium, receptivity, sensitivity, cooperation, compromise and working together. The Two is the first vibration of the nine basic numbers which addresses social issues for, in progression, the One is now moving beyond itself into the domain of duality and discovering that other people, other entities, other points of view, other philosophies, other cultures and so forth do exist, and in order to live harmoniously and in balance with one another, one must consider and embrace other <u>Ones</u> as well as itself. As John Donne said, "No man is an island." It is the Two Lifepath in which this thought comes to life and showers lessons upon the individual so that the reality of others is received and embraced.

When a person is born into the Two Lifepath, the life will be spent in a support capacity. Under this vibration, the lesson is not necessarily to lead but to follow, maintain, corroborate and support those in the lead. Although society often gives over-enthusiastic high praise to leadership, followership is just as important. After all, without followers there could be no leaders. And without efficient, competent, strong, dedicated, devoted, intelligent, loving support, nothing could ever get done by those who may have the vision but not the wherewithal to accomplish or carry out the plan or the task at hand.

For example, although officers are the decision makers in the Army and all armed forces, it has been said that, "Sergeants run the Army, not officers." In other words, it is the sergeants who, after receiving orders from their commanding officers, implement those orders and insure their execution. In like manner, it can also be said that secretaries, not presidents or chairmen, run the business world. Like sergeants, they are the ones responsible for carrying out the plan and seeing that the detail work is done. Just a little thought here will reveal how precious and uncompromisingly critical a sergeant, secretary or support person can be to the success or failure of any enterprise. As the yin and yang form an integrated whole, so leaders and followers must work together in the concept of wholeness. Neither can exist without the other. Therefore, although the Two Lifepath is one of support, it is by no means unimportant. Nor should one think less of himself or herself if either is placed in a support role. After all, from a purely spiritual point of view there is only one Commander in Chief and the rest of creation exists to serve Him and His Plan.

In the Two Lifepath, music may well be a major aspect of the life experience. All rhythm is composed of an up-stroke and a down-stroke - a two-stroke cycle. Reflective of this concept is point-counterpoint, consonance-dissonance, fast-slow tempos, etc., all factors which create contrast in music and appreciation of one factor for the other. Generally speaking, women have more natural musical rhythm than men. It is no coincidence that women are ruled by the Two vibration and men by the One vibration, the latter lacking in the bi-polar ingredient to make it rhythmical. This is not to say that men do not have rhythm. It is to say that it is the female principle in Nature that engenders rhythm more than the masculine ray. Furthermore, 'feminine' does not necessarily mean 'effeminate' either, although one who is strongly feminine will naturally be effeminate. All of us, whether we are male or female, have some aspect of the opposing polar energy in us, just as in the yin/yang symbol of the ancient Tao where there is a white dot in the black hemisphere and a black dot in the white hemisphere. Within the masculine, there is feminine; within the feminine, there is masculine. Nothing is totally black or white, positive or negative in this dimension of duality.

The positive aspect of the Two Lifepath is perfect balance and loving support. The number Two represents duality. This duality is further represented by the teeter-totter going up and down, just as the pendulum sways back and forth and the ocean's tides flow in and out. When each of these actions is given its proper respect, measure and attention, there is perfect balance.

Harmony, peace and love will result. When an over-emphasis is placed on one polarity or the other, imbalance occurs. Strife, struggle and discomfort are the result. It is difficult to achieve balance because we often spend too much time focusing on one polarity or the other. The issues of self importance often stand in the way. Pride and ego create imbalance by not recognizing others, others of all kinds - people, issues, concerns, feelings, animals, etc.

It is the Two Lifepath which brings into focus these issues and concepts of others. Hence, qualities of compassion, consideration, compromise, cooperation, companionship, togetherness (as opposed to "I-ness"), diplomacy, patience, tolerance, kindness, giving, sweetness, harmony, and equilibrium become the positive focus of this lifescript.

On the negative side of this Two Lifepath is destructive imbalance and contention. Since Two rules 'others', the individual will be placed in life arenas, circumstances, situations, environments and predicaments where he or she can learn and experience what this 'others concept' is all about. Often, competition is found within this vibratory field, for it is competition which places one against other ones in a field of comparison and contrast, i.e., the playing field, the court, the debate facility, the forum, the legislature, etc. Learning neither to dominate nor subordinate is the ultimate goal in this arena. Rather, it is to cooperate and compromise for the peace and balance of all. Oftentimes, we see strong egos in the competitive arenas of life and it is this competitive arena which exists to lift the ego-driven soul into a place of balance and harmony where winning and losing, victory and defeat are each seen in their proper perspective - as opposite polarities of the same issue. Ultimately, each is insignificant and one must learn under this Two Lifepath vibration that the ultimate winner is neither the victor nor the vanquished, but the balanced! Why? Because where there is balance one can walk the tightrope of life without falling off and jeopardizing his life or the lives of others and cross the chasm of life from beginning to end successfully, continuing in the journey of one's spiritual evolution.

Thus, under this Two Lifepath, one must be aware of competition taken to levels of unhealthy contention, confliction and war. Absolutely no good will come or can come from a situation in which dominance, not tolerance, is the end result. When the pendulum swings one way, it must by its very nature swing the other. No one wins forever. The way of the warrior is death. He who wins will lose and he who loses will win. It's as axiomatic as the rising and falling of the tide, as certain as the inflow and outflow of air to and from the lungs, as predictable as the coming and going of the seasons.

Another caution of the Two Lifepath is the possibility of negative duplicity, deceit and deception. Because Two represents polar extremes, it is easy under this vibration to show two sides, one true; one false. Showing two sides can be deceitful and the deception generated will create negative karma and guarantee its return to its 'generator'. Here again, balance is the key, for in a balanced state, one can see both sides of the teeter-totter at once because it is straight and true - one line with two aspects but in one elevation.

In life, there are sins of omission as well as sins of co-mission. Because Two is dual by nature, there is the distinct possibility in this lifepath of vacillation, of swaying back and forth and not coming to a definitive conclusion. Hence, one can become bogged down and make no progress vis-à-vis definitive action. Vacillation may be good at times, but it can also cause problems. Thus, under this Two Lifepath, it is suggested that one learn not to vacillate if such vacillation generates an imbalance thwarting success. Again, it is best that the teeter-totter remain still and balanced so that there may not be any chaos or disruption caused by a state of imbalance.

The positive lesson for the Two Lifepath is, therefore, balance. Where balance exists, the energies of life flow smoothly and freely for everyone to share and experience equally. Imbalance may create excitement, but it can never create peace.

Because Two rules support and governs women in general, it is natural that oftentimes throughout history it has been a woman who has been "the power behind the throne." Simply because Two rules support it does not mean that Two is less intelligent than the One. Leaders are not necessarily smarter than followers. They may have more directorial presence, more will to survive, more arrogance, more ego involvement but these do not equate to intelligence. Therefore, leaders must not patronize followers or speak down to them but rather seek their support and be grateful they have it.

Beginning in the year 2000, the world entered a thousand years of Two energy - the energy of the Yin, the female. Therefore, the current millennium will be very different from the last thousand years marked by the number One - the Yang, the male. For more on this subject, read *The Age of the Female: A Thousand Years of Yin* and *The Age of the Female II: Heroines of the Shift* available at www.richardking.net.

The 3 Lifepath

As One represents the yang, the male principle of Nature and Two, the yin, the female principle, Three personifies their union, their blending and integration. Spiritually, Three denotes the Trinity, the Divine Relationship of Father, Son, and Holy Ghost; Master, Disciple, Word. On a different level, the trinity is reflected in other structures such as body-mind-spirit; man-woman-marriage; father-mother-child; concept-materialization-expression.

Therefore, the Three Lifepath is one which focuses on this triune relationship and its different forms. On a personal level the Three, represented by the triangle - the symbol of perfection, manifests itself through individual expression in many forms - physically as beauty and health; mentally through the creative arts, especially those dealing with words; socially as good times with friends; romantically as marriage or intimate relationship.

As we can see, the Three Lifepath is rooted in the vibration of self-expression and personal integration. If there is a preponderance of Three energy in the chart beyond the lifepath itself, the more intense the expressive factors will be. Invariably, concentrated Three energy means a lifescript where words may play a major role in some type of communicative activity, interest or employment. This may translate to a career in writing, art, law, language, teaching, acting, singing, reporting, commentating, etc.

It may also equate to careers in health and beauty where personal integration with the body is important, or in a modeling career where one uses the body as the vehicle of self-expression.

Generally speaking, the Three Lifepath affords the easiest and most fulfilling of all the life scripts. Because it is the vibration of integration and expression, people are usually more happy and relaxed under its influence. There is, as compared with the other life lessons, little stress with this Three sojourn through life. If any lifepath vibration could be called the 'vacation lifepath', it would be the Three. This energy field generally brings ease, pleasure, good times, friends and overall enjoyment. Of course, it does have its problems like all life scripts. This dimension in which we live is not paradise and is not problem free. Everybody dies. Everybody gets sick from time to time. Everyone experiences stress. However, the intensity of life's problems have a tendency to be mitigated under this vibratory pattern and problems just don't seem to carry the weight and burden they can carry compared with other numerical vibrations.

The triangle, the geometric symbol of the Three, integrates. When there is a positive connection between the three apexes of the triangle, there is free-flowing expression and fulfillment because the energy of the vibration is flowing within a completed circuit. But if the circuit is broken, disruption occurs and the expression becomes negatively aspected. Therefore, the other side of the coin for the Three is not integration but disintegration. Where there was health on one side of the coin, there is now sickness. Where there was positive self-expression, there is now self-destruction. Where there was the positive usage of words, there is now the negative usage of words and language. Where there were friends, there are now enemies. This will not happen, however, unless the chart is negatively aspected or if the person becomes too self-indulgent, self-centered, self-consumed, entitled and arrogant, which is a possibility with this vibration since it is so highly charged with self-expression.

When we experience our selves being expressive to a high level, there is always the possibility we will get a big head and lose perspective of our true place in the cosmos. We must always remember that everything we own actually belongs to God, not to us, and He may, at any time and for any reason, take back or destroy that which He gives freely to us to use but not to claim and, certainly, not to flaunt. Nothing in this universe belongs to us, including our creativity, beauty, health and self-expression, and if we begin thinking that it does, we may just be in for a very rude awakening. Thus, we should enjoy the Three vibration and embrace it but not flaunt it, abuse it, or take it for granted, emitting an attitude of entitlement and arrogance.

The admonition here is that the Three Lifepath, being one primarily of self-expression and personal integration, should be used positively to promote one's spiritual integration. Negative expression, or a saturation of material and mortal expression, will do nothing for the soul but move it down the ladder of life, not up the ladder of life where eternal and supernal pleasure exist in contrast to the temporal pleasure of this material universe. Nothing lasts forever in this dimension, and when the great cosmic pendulum swings to one polarity, it will, by natural law, swing to the opposite one. Thus, a life of great ease, comfort, pleasure and beauty lived now in this incarnation, may give way to a life of great hardship, discomfort, pain and ugliness in another. It is the way of life in this dimension. Therefore, the greatest good that an individual can accomplish under the ease of this Three Lifepath is not to become complacent but to work diligently toward one's sense of divine integration. At its zenith, the Three Lifepath directly addresses an integrated connection with all that is divine, spiritual, ethereal and eternal. This is the higher ground for this vibration and the wise person will follow its road. . . uphill.

Yet, if used inappropriately the Three energy will force the individual downhill, often in an uncontrolled spiral of self-destruction, self-mutilation, self-degradation, disease, dis-ease, drug and sexual abuse. The number Three rules pleasure as well as its flip side, disease. Too much carnal pleasure such as alcoholic consumption, recreational drug use, sexual indulgence and culinary intemperance will create an imbalance leading to sickness and disease.

Another caution of the Three misuse is ego-saturation and entitlement. While the number One rules identity, the number Three rules image, and an image carried to the extreme point of excessive vanity creates a maelstrom of problems. A study of the lives of those individuals whose egos are commonly viewed as quite large, who carry a sense of entitlement, and who are infatuated with themselves will verify this fact.

Because Three rules words and communication, the Three Lifepath may well give its owner experiences reflecting both positive and negative words and communication such as expressions of love and hate, support and interference, harmony and anger. Expect both with this lifepath but keep balanced throughout the journey. Keep in mind, too, that Three rules health and disease, so it's best to focus on the health issues and avoid the excesses that create not only physical disease but mental and emotional dis-ease.

The number Three also rules children, so the Three Lifepath may well bring issues of children into focus. Depending on other aspects in the numerology chart, these may be good or bad. Positive aspects would be the support, encouragement and honoring of children and their well-being. Negative aspects would be child neglect and abuse including but not limited to emotional abuse, sexual abuse and physical abuse.

Ultimately, the highest goal of the Three Lifepath is to express Divine Expression and gratitude for all things while remaining humble for the gifts given. In many ways, this journey through the Three territory offers a rest for the soul and mind. It is a journey, however, that must not be abused, taken for granted nor disrespected lest it be taken away.

The 4 Lifepath

The Four Lifepath addresses everything related to structure - physical structure, spiritual structure, emotional structure, mental structure, marital structure, material structure, employment structure, social structure, creative structure, financial structure, and foundational structure. Obviously, the key word for the Four is *structure* and a lifescript maintaining this energy field will deal in the arena of *form*.

Some of the key words for the Four vibration are earth, work, effort, toil, service, discipline, control, construction, destruction, devotion, rules, order, persistence, resistance, recalcitrance, practicality, rationality, determination, fidelity, loyalty, security, regimentation, restriction, limitation, strength, tradition, convention, conservatism, roots, groundedness, anchoring, solidity, matter and materialism.

A Four Lifepath will be one of constancy and little change. Four is strong but it does not like to move, be adventurous or explore new things. Four likes to stay right where it is. It loves roots and avoids being uprooted in any way - physically, mentally, spiritually, socially, emotionally, financially, etc. Four loves to be secure because it is the vibration of security.

Because the Four energy plants itself in one place, a person under this vibration would do well in situations and environments where there is little change and, in fact, the life under this vibration will not be filled with much change at all unless there is a dominant amount of Five energy elsewhere in the chart. The person may change and be changeable; his or her nature may be changeable, but the Four Lifepath calls for a grounding, a sense of stability, a rootedness in life or lessons involving stability and rootedness where there exists a fair amount of transformation or a changing and metamorphosis of form.

Because the lifepath is the structure dealing with life lessons, the person living the Four Lifepath will be forced, voluntarily or involuntarily, to learn the importance of structure in life, relationships, activities and projects. There will be toil under this vibration, constant and enduring effort. One will be placed in situations where issues broached will relate to discipline, devotion, fidelity, constancy, work, effort, reliability, service and security.

Because Four is symbolically represented by the square, one may find himself either confined within the walls of the square, as if imprisoned, or standing on top of the square, free from the confining limitations of the square but, nonetheless, rooted, grounded, magnetized, stuck, even chained to it.

The positive thing about the Four is that it is solid. The negative thing about the Four is that it is solid, sometimes too solid for its own good. In effect, its asset is its liability. Life changes, and if one is to be successful in life, one must be willing or able to change with the times, tides or events of life's ever changing currents. If one cannot change, or if one doesn't want to move when he or she should move, or refuses to move, one may come to severe harm, even die for being too solid, i.e. too stubborn for one's own good. It is good to be strong. It is good to be faithful. It is good to be secure. It is good to be disciplined. It is good to be controlled. But it is not good to be anchored to the ground when a hundred foot tidal wave is rapidly approaching and one refuses to move in stubborn defiance of the laws of Nature and in celebration of man's strength and courage. Such stubbornness is not strength; nor is it courage. It is glaring and lethal stupidity. Discretion is the better part of valor, and if there is a fault to the wonderful stability of the Four, it is that it does not recognize when it should move, change and alter the conditions of its form. Even snakes shed their skin. So must we all if we're to grow and evolve.

The positive aspect of the Four Lifepath has solid, spiritual import. Spiritual success is founded upon purity of the spirit. Purity of the spirit cannot be achieved unless one exercises discipline, sacrifice, restraint and control over the internal and external forces of the world which are constantly urging and importuning the individual to be undisciplined, unrestrained, uncontrolled, unfaithful, if not down right wanton and dissolute. Thus, it is good to be rooted in the onslaught of such negativity, otherwise, one might well be destabilized, moved off course, and, thereby, denied the opportunity of achieving spiritual success which is generated and achieved by strength, courage, determination, sacrifice and an absolute conviction and set of actions, behaviors and conducts which do not betray its manifestation.

Squares have sharp corners and defined edges. While this can be an advantage in some circumstances, having sharp edges in a social instance can be damaging to all parties. Because Fours can be stubborn and resistant, it's advisable to, when appropriate, soften the corners and edges of the square, being more forgiving, less stubborn, less dogmatic, less opinionated. Therefore, the admonition of the Four is: "Be strong but have a soft and tender heart."

The lesson of the Four Lifepath is to learn to be constant, faithful, devoted, strong, courageous, determined, unrelenting, hard-working, service-oriented and secure. Be the rock. Be solid and enduring, but. . . have enough sense to move and comprise when it is appropriate and insure the edges of the square are soft and harmless when they need to be.

Your Love Numbers   King

The 5 Lifepath

The Five Lifepath is the most fluid of the nine basic life scripts. Under this vibration, there is constant motion, movement, change, exploration, shifting, variety, diversity, detachment and freedom. Whereas the Four lifepath is one of roots and stability, the Five Lifepath is almost devoid of roots unless they are in the wind. The Five Lifepath will definitely bring change to the person's life and such change will be intensified if it is corroborated by other Five energy in the chart. Do not think of big, stable, secure rocks with this vibration. This is the energy of the wind, the constant ever-changing tide action of the sea, and the amorphous form of mercury on the move.

The Five Lifepath gives the freedom of movement so longed for by the one rooted and bound by the walls of the Four and who longs for a less restricted life. But too much change, too much movement, too much variety, too much freedom can be a prison in itself, an ever-changing hurricane where one longs for some anchoring, some stillness and security in the dynamic motion of the wind. As the English Romantic poet, Richard Lovelace, wrote in his poem *To Althea, From Prison*: "Stone walls do not a prison make, nor iron bars a cage. . ." Certainly, every lifepath has its freedoms as well as its prisons, and the walls and bars of the prison come in many forms, sizes, shapes and intensities.

One of the challenges of the Five Lifepath is managing the coming and going of events, people, projects, activities, fortunes and relationships, for all of these have a habit of changing regularly and often. This creates a sense of uncertainty because nothing ever seems to stick, to stay in place, to remain still. But it's not supposed to. The great lesson of this lifepath is freedom, but not in the way we normally think of freedom. All of the movement, change and motion of the Five Lifepath is designed to detach us from that which anchors us down and paralyzes us. At its apex, the Five Lifepath exists to detach us totally from the world and the material dimension, allowing our soul the experience of absolute freedom in spiritual transcendence.

Normally, we think of freedom as the ability to do whatever we want, whenever we want. But this definition is restricted because true freedom demands great discipline, great control, great restraint and great regulation. The Five Lifepath gives us a certain level of unrestricted movement, action, fun, friends, a variety of opportunities and enjoyable experiences to see if we can truly learn the lesson of what freedom really is. True freedom is the total absence of attachment to the world of form and absolute obedience, even slavery, to the Will of God. The enigma is that when we live in His Will, although we are His slave, we are truly free, for nothing can then restrict us in this dimension or in any dimension because we live in the divine Will of God. We come and go at will, unhampered by the fetters of the senses, faces, places and races of the creation. Why? Because we move in Him and He is omnipotent. As a drop of water we have, in effect, merged with the ocean of God. Therefore, when we attach ourselves to the Divine Will, we move in the power of His omnipotence. What could be more free?

We can think of this freedom issue in another way. If one wishes to be a concert pianist, one does not simply sit down at the keyboard and play staggeringly beautiful and exquisite music.

Such great piano talent, such total freedom, comes at the expense of almost ruthless incarceration within the walls of discipline, practice, determination, restriction, constriction and long-suffering. There is a price to pay for real freedom, and that price is not freedom, is it slavery, slavery to that regimentation, restraint, discipline, control and toil that sets us free. Any great artist can testify to the horrendously long and tedious hours of practice and patience where there was no freedom of escape from the torment of creating the skill necessary to be free. A great musician can generate great music with effortless effort in a rich tapestry of complete freedom, but such freedom was the child of adherence to rules and regulation, not their absence. This is the great lesson of the Five Lifepath - great freedom is the child of slavery. Such beautiful irony.

At the earthly level, the vibration of the Five Lifepath often places its students squarely in the middle of the Valley of the Senses. When residing here, the mistake is to think that this is a time, place and opportunity for saturating one's experience in sensual pursuit. Nothing could be further from the truth. This is the time to learn that resistance from overt sensual experience is liberating, that indulgence in such experience, which is what is most commonly perceived, does not lead to freedom but material and carnal bondage. It is in this Five Lifepath that the soul is placed in this 'Valley of the Senses' and given a choice to see if it can truly learn freedom or be captivated and imprisoned by a false concept of it.

Thus, not only is great strength required of those who walk the Five Lifepath and who would be free, but they must also maintain a strong sense of discernment and discretion. Within the incarnation of this Five life script, situations will be placed before the individual in which tough choices will have to be made regarding the health and progress of the soul. Restriction or indulgence will be the fabric of these choices, and whatever the choices made, there will be consequences because freedom is not action devoid of consequence. Freedom is action taken in awareness, acceptance and consideration of consequence.

For example, under the energy veil of the Five Lifepath, people may think they can do whatever they like and that freedom has no boundaries, no limitations, no restrictions, no consequences. And because Five rules the senses and diverse experiences, if people adopt this non-consequential philosophy they may become too involved in the indulgences of drugs, sex, gambling and other activities which ultimately enslave them, leading them into a valley of despair rather than into the supernal skies of spiritual freedom and liberation. It's always a two-edged sword with numbers, just like everything in this duality-based creation.

Within the framework of the Five Lifepath, one will come in contact with a large number and variety of people. Thus, one's experiences will be enlarged and expanded. As Five is the numerical vibration which rules the senses, it is also the 'Number of Man'. Therefore, Five can be translated into the single word, "people", and under the Five veil, there will come and go many people, many relationships, many experiences. A person with a Five life script will find his or her life's vocations (plural on purpose) concentrated in those jobs and areas of employment which cater to and deal with many people.

Another aspect of the Five Lifepath is the variety of talents the person will possess. Five rules variety and the Five's mercurial energy will grant opportunities to use many talents in many ways. Remember, in all ways, Five moves. It does not remain concentrated or fixed to one thing or activity. This can be exciting and stimulating and, certainly, the Five Lifepath is never boring. Fast cars, fast boats, fast planes, fast horses, dancing, marital arts - anything pertaining to motion and movement come under the umbrella of the Five vibration.

Buddha said that attachment is the root of all suffering because when we're attached to something or someone and we lose it or them, we suffer. The Five energy is designed to detach us from the shackles of this world and make us free by giving us so much change that we learn not to cling to things, people, events, conditions, pets, interests, etc. True freedom equates to total detachment, never attachment unless it is to God. Of all the nine major lifepaths, it is the Five Lifepath which teaches us this lesson of detachment leading to true, spiritual freedom. Furthermore, this freedom is not based in a theory of "license carte blanche" but in discipline and control, reflecting the powerful words of the famed Pythagoras: "No man is free who cannot control himself."

The 6 Lifepath

Heart. Hearth. Home. Personal love. Devotion. Domesticity. Community. Beauty. Adjustments. Responsibility. Nurturing.

These are characteristics of the Six Lifepath and an individual transiting this lifepath will be involved in all that involves "ticker," the beating of the heart from romance to relatives, home and community.

Six, a higher octave of the Two, is potentially the warmest and most loving of all the basic numbers. Positively expressed, it reflects that which is soft, sweet, tender, gentle, kind, caring, tolerant, patient, nurturing, supportive and harmonizing. The Six demonstrates these qualities primarily in the home and community environments. Individuals with this Six Lifepath will, no doubt, be heavily engaged in caring for others [people and animals], parenting and parenthood, and the bulk of the life lessons will center in and around the family and domestic environment.

A person with a Six Lifepath will be learning about the Six energy. This is a critical point regarding the lifepath vibration because the lifepath focuses on learning and being involved with its vibration. It doesn't mean the person himself naturally exudes the number characteristics identifying the lifepath. "Exuded qualities" would be found in the individual's name at birth, the Expression, which is discussed in the following chapter. Qualities of the lifepath vibration are learned qualities, not exuded qualities. Therefore, having a Six Lifepath doesn't necessarily mean a person will express the qualities of the Six on a personal level, although lifepath energies may cause one to acquire and manifest their essence in some way. As we recall, the lifepath is the script of someone's life. It is not the actor [the person] living life from the core of his being. It is rather life being lived, i.e. acted out, through a script - the lifepath. As we look upon the lifepath as the "hand" we were dealt at birth which must be played out, or as the curriculum of our life which must be studied, we realize that 'studied' or 'learned' qualities, although possibly being incipient in the life because of the lifepath energy, may not necessarily be inherent in the person. This is an important distinction when analyzing a person's life.

In the Six Lifepath one will generally learn to make others happy, do for them, support them, love and nurture them. In its highest expression, the Six Lifepath is about unconditional, personal love. On the other hand, it can reflect a life of personal, selfish gain and irresponsibility. Because it can be loving, the caution is for the individual not to sacrifice himself beyond what is individually healthy; not to become so nurturing he or she becomes a doormat allowing people to walk over him or her.

This Six Lifepath vibration often involves music - the giving of love through melodious sound. Many musicians and singers have Sixes dominant in their charts. Beauty and art can also come under this cipher, especially the type of beauty that is loving and harmonious, sweetly flowing and warmly pleasing.

Because Six rules the domestic environment, occupations involving the home and community come into focus. Nurses, teachers, doctors, interior decorators, architects, landscapers, gardeners, homecare practitioners, childcare specialists, insurance agents and community organizers are some of the careers contained within the Six milieu.

Sex is also a major function of the Six vibration because it is the sharing of personal, physical love. Unfortunately, this love is often degraded into less than the true, caring, physical, emotional and psychological interaction that it represents in its highest expression and becomes lust instead. Sex may be an expression of physical love, but sex is not love and love is not sex, nor is the phrase "making love" a true manifestation of love in its highest form. When love is equated to sex, the sanctity of love is lost.

The polar opposite of love is hate. Thus, with the Six Lifepath it would not be unusual for one to experience hate, anger, jealousy, envy and bitterness at some point during the life. Individuals manifesting a spiritual outlook in life will be loving, kind, considerate, tolerant, sweet, and harmonious. However, those with less than a spiritual outlook, and bent on fulfilling love's negative side, will no doubt be more prone to expressing the energy of hate, intolerance, inharmony and unkindness. This is why it is critical to have a spiritual outlook in life and, furthermore, a life which manifests spirituality in action and deed, not merely in words. Where hate is present, discord, disease, destruction and death prevail. One cannot be high-minded and lead a low life. One simply cannot live in the fire of hell and feel the soothing, sweet ambrosial waters of heaven. If we want love, peace, harmony and beauty in our lives, then we must generate these energies as we live day to day, not hope or wish for them while living in and manifesting a life of contrary and antagonistic values and actions. The Law of Karma is exact: we reap the fruit of the seeds we sow. Until we live this law in a spiritually positive manner, we will continue to suffer from and experience the energies of hate, intolerance, anger, disease, discord and inharmony.

Given the sacred subject of love, a person with a Six Lifepath has much important work to do in focusing upon and manifesting love, true love. Six can be a wonderfully warm, nurturing and spiritual vibration but its manifestation requires purity of thought, purity of motive, purity of action, purity of commitment, purity of duty, purity of devotion, purity of promise. As 16th Century, Saint Dadu, stated: "Hold pure, stay pure, say pure, take the pure, give the pure." It's impossible to miss the operative word in Dadu's statement. When thought, motive and action are muddied and adulterated, love is not pure and loses its sweet nurturing essence, potentially turning vile with discord and hate. Therefore, it's critical to be purely focused with the Six Lifepath. No vibration is sweeter or more loving when given the care and concern it deserves and demands.

The 7 Lifepath

The Seven Lifepath is the royal highway to spirituality. It is the path of spiritual testing, the vein that does not lead to gold but to Light. It is the doorway to the inner worlds. It moves one from a consciousness of reality to Reality. There is no other vibration more potent for quickening the spirit than the Seven. It does not make a man rich. It makes a man enlightened. Those who follow this path are possibly in for, not the ride of their lives, but the ride of their existence. Seven is the secret tube leading up and in and out - up the stairway of the consciousness, in through the secret passageway of the Third Eye and out of this material dimension of duality and darkness into the inner regions of refulgent Light and Sound.

In order to make this inward journey, one must be removed from the outer world of confusion and chaos; removed from the hustle and bustle of buzzing bees relentlessly toiling and foraging to fashion their honeyed hives; removed from the dissonant sounds and cacophonous cries of the materially minded and worldly wise; removed from all that is external and loud and distracting and noisy and coarse and crude and false in order that one may have the opportunity to listen to the still small voice within so that he may, if he is extremely fortunate, catch the Divine Celestial Current and follow the Sound and Light Home to where all is calm, warm, peaceful, blissful, loving and . . . Real. It is the Seven which does this removing.

However, as majestic, grand, noble and spiritual as this lifepath can be, it does not come without a price. The price is often pain, tragedy, heartache, heartbreak, agony, loneliness, betrayal, ignominy, dishonor, long-suffering, extreme frustration and misfortune with a capital 'M'. As 20th Century Saint, Charan Singh, has stated: "For getting the highest thing in life, we have to pay the highest price." The cost of moving into the inner worlds is the release, the giving up, the letting go of the outer worlds and all they represent and reflect. These opposing worlds - the inner and the outer, are totally incompatible. One cannot live in both. It is either one or the other. And as another 20th Century Saint, Sawan Singh, has said: the spiritual path is "death in life; a living death." Seven is the cipher of the spiritual path. It is the path of death to the material world and birth into the inner worlds.

In order to begin this inner quest of the spirit, we must endure a detaching from that which is material. This is difficult for most of us because we have been transiting the outer worlds of flesh and form for eons in countless incarnations, and our consciousness has grown accustomed to the external illusion to such a degree that we resemble barnacles stuck to the wet, storm-worn, weather-washed rock walls of the material monolith we call earthly existence. But to follow the inner path, we must be pried free of our tenacious attachment and carnal cohesion. Therefore, along comes the Seven to sever these binding bonds by giving us solitude to reflect on life, isolation to protect us from the insidious nature of others, heartache and heartbreak to move us away from worldly loves to His love, betrayal to cut the ties to those unworthy of our love, ignominy and dishonor to teach us humility, disease to teach us tranquility, and long-suffering to make us wait . . . and burn . . . and become pure.

Unfortunately, many souls who are living the Seven Lifepath miss the point. Rather than turn inward to find the way out - for the way out is in, they continue to run out, seeking solace for their problems by clinging harder to the very rock which anchors them to this nether land and from which they must break away to be free. Alcoholism is one way some souls choose to find peace from the detaching turmoil of their existence. Untoward relationships are another. Drugs still another. Such souls drown their suffering in these poisons which only further poison their lives and, ultimately, lead to additional pain and suffering. However, there comes a time in the development of the spiritual self when it must learn to be patient and endure its suffering, not attempt to mask it or run away from it, because it is the suffering that purifies, and purity is the essential essence of the Spirit. To be one with the

Spirit, one must be pure and to be pure most of us must endure the fires of purification which suffering brings. In its highest purpose, life is not about comfort. It is about God Realization, and it is no easy thing to make the transition from a worldly-centered life to a God-centered one. But . . . if we're to achieve our spiritual liberation, it must be done. Hence, the soul is graced with the Seven energy and its characteristics of isolation, patience, tolerance, calmness, quietude, reclusiveness, separation, suffering, tragedy, misfortune, chaos and calamity to assist us in this divine process.

In social gatherings, when others are mixing and interacting, it is the Seven which stands or sits off to the side - alone, quiet, pensive, seemingly distant and cool. Seven is not a social mixer. It is an internal dweller. It thinks, reflects, cogitates, meditates, muses, observes, questions and analyzes. For externally focused souls, it may be "hip and happening" to be socially gregarious, but for the indwelling Seven, it's all happening on the inside, and socializing is as dull and boring to it as the inner existence is to those seeking social interaction. Individuals with a Seven Lifepath can therefore expect to be placed in settings and environments where they are isolated and separated, giving them an opportunity for reflection and self-examination.

Sometimes, being and feeling alone and separated from the masses, Sevens may worry and think themselves odd and strange. To others they may also seem odd and strange. From a worldly perspective, it is understandable that they would be considered different but they should not worry about this because they are not different from those who inhabit the inner kingdoms, which is where the astute Seven is headed. An admonition for the Seven is, "Forget the world and its external, outer, material, social path. It is not your way. Yours is the other way. The inner way. The way in. Therefore, go within and there you will find your destiny and your peace."

The Seven Lifepath is, ironically, the most chaotic and the most peaceful; the most glorious and the most inglorious; the most enlightened and the most darkened, the most noble and the most ignoble of all the lifepaths. It is in this life script that the two edged sword wields its razor-sharp edges with poignant and painful precision, cutting through the illusion of this material reality by severing the powerful magnetic chains which bind us to it. Although Seven can bring great peace and tranquility, that peace is usually the result of great stress, trial, tribulation, isolation, sorrow, pain, suffering, anxiety, frustration and disruption. When one lives in 'heat' for extended periods, one learns to adjust to it, accept it and remain calm and unaffected by it. After all, diamonds are made under extreme heat and pressure over extended periods of time, not by a mere and casual blowing of an intermittent wind. If we're to be diamonds and reflect the refulgent brilliance of the Light, we will have to be baked and pressured in the furnace of the world. This is not a pleasant experience, but the result is that we become a diamond in the process, a price worth paying when we eventually look back at the dirty, dark, comparatively worthless coal mine of a world we once called home.

Seven, the most sacred of all numbers, rules both saints and sinners. On one side of its coin, it reflects total chaos. On the other, total bliss. The metaphor of the hurricane is a perfect depiction of the Seven Lifepath - destructive outer winds circling a perfectly calm center. Its message: when we experience the tumultuous winds of life, the key is to use their force to force us inward to the center, to the eye of the storm, the center of our purest being where all is calm, peaceful and still, following the spiritual directive, "Be still, and know that I am God" (Bible: Psalm 46:10).

The admonishment for those on the Seven Lifepath - Go Within. Don't fight the battle on the outside. The way out is in. You must fight the battle on the Inside. This is what the Seven is forcing you to do, so do it! Do not mask or cover your frustration, pain or sorrow with intoxicant stimulants and negative acts which poison your mind and spirit and inhibit you from feeling the very heat, fire and pressure which exist to cleanse and purify your mind and spirit, making you fit to receive and transmit light to a darkened world. The Seven Lifepath is the door to great mystical, magical, spiritual illumination. Allow it to work to lift you to the zenith of your greatest ethereal good - the refulgent, luminescent being that is the Child of the Light!

Child of the Light

You are a Child of the Light,
a coruscating spire of white-fire flame,
a vortex of white-fire sun;
a crystalline spray of white-fire ray,
a soul whose time has come.

The universe beckons and God demands
you radiate your Light through space,
fusing your power this very hour,
illuminating the magnificence of your race,
a race where man is all in one,
non-separate and complete,
a single soul, in total, whole,
with multiple hands and feet.

Souls emerge and now converge
in a world approaching Dawn.
In inner space they see a race
where splendor flows in song;
where white-fire light inspires
and radiates the cosmic core,
where Beings rise in azure skies
to live forevermore.

Yes, you are a Child of the Light,
a coruscating spire of white-fire flame,
a vortex of white-fire sun,

a crystalline spray of white-fire ray,
a soul whose time has come.

So cast white-fire higher;
let consciousness rise to see;
let soul explore the secret door
that leads to infinity.
The time is now. The space is here.
Excuse yourself no more.
Radiate Light, extinguish night
and live forevermore.

For you are a Child of the Light,
a coruscating spire of white-fire flame,
a vortex of white-fire sun,
a crystalline spray of white-fire ray,
a soul whose time has come.

The 8 Lifepath

The Eight Lifepath is the script of interaction, connection, disconnection, circulation, orchestration, coordination, commerce, management and all that is involved in the principle of *flow*, be it smooth or rough, graceful or clumsy, swift or slow. Eight connects polarities: positive to negative; male to female; buyer to seller; management to labor; concept to completion; product to consumer; past to present. Traditionally, the Eight has been regarded as a money number. But in reality it is not. Money, ruled by the number Two, is the ingredient, the substance of the *flow* of commerce but it is not the flow itself. Eight is the flow.

The Eight Lifepath is about interactive efficiency. The energies of this life script will manifest many circumstances, conditions, events, problems and people into the life of the person in order to teach him or her what works and does not work in making life successful, not just in business or commerce, but in social, domestic, personal and professional arenas.

The Eight cipher is unique. When turned on its side it becomes the ancient lemniscate representing infinity, beautifully symbolizing the flow of energy between polarities.

The Lemniscate Eight Loop

Positive Pole [+]  [-] Negative Pole

As Seven is the most intrinsic of vibrations, Eight is the most extrinsic, the highest octave of the external social quatrain of the vibrations 2-4-6-8. Eight likes to mix, manage, mingle, manipulate, orchestrate, interact, involve and connect. It is not generally a deep, mystical, reflective, thoughtful number. It is, however, a powerfully social and commercially connective number. What Seven is to the inner worlds, Eight is to the outer worlds, for it flows and connects and/or disconnects people, energies, ideas and things of one polarity to other people, energies, ideas and things of the opposite polarity.

Eight and Seven are opposites. Eight loves to mix, seek the outer world of material success, wealth, riches, property, titles and all the accouterments and status money can bring. Eight generally cares little about the inner worlds, inner realities and activities requiring introspection. Seven, on the other hand, is an odd number. It is inward-seeking, private, reclusive, reflective, introverted and introspective, shying away from too much socializing and worldly activity. The Seven seeks solitude and does not care much for the outer display of the material world. In the lifepath position, the Seven will force the individual into some aspect of separation, isolation or seclusion.

Those souls who carry Eight as a life lesson, therefore, will be compelled to focus their attention generally on external, social, worldly, material matters. But not always. There are exceptions to every rule. As every number has a positive and negative polarity, so does it have a spiritual and material aspect as well. Eight can be a very spiritual number, seeking to make a connection between God and man, the inner worlds and outer worlds. But, generally, Eight can be thought of as worldly. Those who are compelled to operate under this vibration can make very good executives, managers, leaders and administrators because the specific function of these positions demands a coordination of all parts of the whole. From top to bottom, low rung to high rung, basement to penthouse, janitor to president, the leader, manager or executive is the one who insures that all is flowing efficiently, smoothly, properly and, hopefully, fairly, humanely and lovingly to assure that the whole organization or institution is successful. And let it be said that the most successful of these individuals will be the ones who see themselves as servants - not bosses, big shots or rulers. The Great Eight works with others to achieve an efficient and harmonious flow within the structure of the organization it serves. And that is the operative word - *serve*, for the Great Eight serves, not subjugates.

High level athletes and performers often carry the Eight cipher in the lifepath. Athletes must be coordinated, and it is the Eight energy that creates a condition of coordination. Having the ability to get the ball in the hoop, the pass to the receiver, the puck in the net, the kick to the target, the parry to the punch, the car to the finish line, the skis over the moguls, the feeling of the song or the meaning of the message to the audience and so forth is all a matter of coordination, orchestration, interaction and connection - a function of Eight energy.

Eight seeks success or that which is traditionally regarded as success - money, social power, recognition, wealth, fame, authority, status, possessions. The non-traditional Eight seeks success in terms of a connection with a higher power. Regardless of the focus, they both want to make that connection which integrates the flow of an idea, impulse or desire with its manifestation, yielding that state of being or accomplishment we regard as success.

Although Eight integrates, administrates and coordinates, it can also manipulate. Eight governs flow. It doesn't govern purity, ethics or morality. It simply moves between polarities, creating connections or disconnections in the process. As money moves through all types of hands, so does the Eight energy move through and between all types of people with all types of motives and intentions. It is only when operating within the sphere of a spiritually elevated consciousness that we can trust the Eight's goodness, sincerity, purpose and truthfulness.

As the actor or actress plays out the Eight Lifepath script, the life lessons will revolve in, through and around the Eight loop - the connective path between polarities. It may be a smooth path, a bumpy path, an intermittent path, but it will be a path of interaction to some degree.

The 9 Lifepath

Nine is the lifepath of the macrocosm, the big picture, the universal stage. In contrast to the personal, loving vibration of the Six, the Nine represents impersonal love. It is compassion, caring, concern, involvement and service in the arena of the 'many', the masses, the public.

Nine often finds itself as the humanitarian, philanthropist, philosopher, teacher, educator, doctor, nurse, singer, actor, writer, performer, volunteer, newscaster. Its universality makes it charismatic, magnetic and attractive but it is not as personally warm and loving as the Six. Nine is public, not personal.

All of the basic numerical digits are encased within the Nine, including the Nine itself. If all the single digits One through Nine are added together, the result is Nine! Because of this aspect, Nine is referred to as the *Grand Elemental*.

$$1 + 2 + 3 + 4 + 5 + 6 + 7 + 8 + 9 = 45 > 4 + 5 = 9$$

Therefore, Nine is all inclusive and complete. It instinctively understands all vibrations, all people. This is why it is popular and charismatic - everyone can identify with it. It is also why Nine 'rules' and is the cipher of sovereignty.

Nine is magical. If it is added to any single digit, that particular digit is duplicated upon reduction. For example:

$$5 + 9 = 14 > 1 + 4 = 5$$
$$8 + 9 = 17 > 1 + 7 = 8$$

Thus, Nine is chameleon-like. It blends with all numbers, all energies, without altering their basic vibration. Therefore, it might be said that Nine is non-judgmental, open-minded and fair.

Because of its chameleon aspect, the Nine faces challenges the other numbers don't. Individuals possessing a Nine Lifepath will be placed in situations where their life will blend with all people. This becomes problematic because the Nine can blend with forces of light or forces of darkness. A person can become absorbed into societies, movements, organizations, groups or cultures that are constructive or destructive; benefic or malefic. Hence, the caution flag must be raised with the Nine.

Because of its universal appeal, Nine often brings fame and fortune. Fame is nothing more than mass recognition, and since everyone can identify with the Nine, it becomes universally known, i.e., famous. In spite of how popular the individual with the Nine Lifepath may or may not be, it is certain that he or she will be involved with the public and the mass of humanity in some way. An individual may even be cast into the limelight. What happens when he gets there is another issue.

As the highest octave of the Three, Nine is extremely artistic, communicative, expressive. With its indigenous, universal energy, it therefore often finds its way to the stage, podium, lens, movie camera, courtroom, classroom, hospital or care center. The Nine Lifepath, because of its universal compassion, may compel one to seek the distant, foreboding environments of the jungle, desert, forest or mountains to help those in need. Nine acts, and usually with compassion unless negatively aspected. After all, in its highest octave, Nine is universal love and love is, itself, a Nine vibration:

$$L \quad O \quad V \quad E$$
$$3 \quad 6 \quad 4 \quad 5 \quad = \quad 18 > \quad 1+8 = \quad 9$$

As love is universal, so is music. The Nine Lifepath often carries one into the profession of music and its performance. No one needs words to understand music because music is felt and experienced. Music is a universal language.

Nine also rules endings, conclusions, completions and terminations. Thus, one with a Nine Lifepath may find himself involved with many endings and finalizations in his life. Perhaps one will even complete a project in this lifetime begun lifetimes earlier in another incarnation. Who knows? Because life is a continuum and reincarnation a reality, this is certainly a plausible concept.

The universal aspect of the Nine Lifepath renders it the perfect vehicle for travel. Individuals playing out this script of life will often find themselves traveling to other places, counties, states, regions or countries.

The main lesson for one with the Nine Lifepath is to be involved with the 'many', the masses, the public. Serve, perform, rule, but do so with great care, responsibility and caution. Karma is never not working in this creation. Great actions bear great reactions and when one is spotlighted on the great stage of life, the consequences can be critical to one's evolution because seeds sewn in the realm of the masses yield massive harvests. If the seeds are good, the harvest will be good. If the seeds are bad, the harvest will be bad. Take heed and act accordingly.

The Lifepath Challenge

Every Lifepath generally contains at least one built-in Challenge - an issue or concern that can be considered a cross we have to bear in life, an obstacle we have to overcome, a problem we have to solve or circumstances requiring careful management.

The Lifepath Challenge is simply determined by subtracting the two ciphers appearing in the binary root structure of the Lifepath from one another. For example, the Lifepath of Mary Jane Smith is a 7; its binary root is 25; its Challenge is 3.

Birth date: 8 January 1960: Lifepath Binary Root is 25 > 7
$8 + 1 + 1 + 9 + 6 + 0 = 25 > 2 + 5 = 7$ Lifepath

$25 > 5$ minus $2 = 3$
Lifepath Challenge is 3

Applying the same formula of subtraction of the Lifepath binaries of John David Doey's Lifepath, we see that his LP Challenge is also a 3.

Birthdate of 14 August 1985: Lifepath Binary Root is 36 > 9

$1 + 4 + 8 + 1 + 9 + 8 + 5 = 36 > 3 + 6 = 9$ Lifepath

36 > 6 minus 3 = 3
Lifepath Challenge is 3

Even though both Mary and John have a 3 Lifepath Challenge, each 3 is derived from a different binary: Mary's from the 25 and John's from the 36. This single number 3 in the Challenge position, derived from a process of subtraction, is called the *Subcap* [the *capstone* from subtraction]. The single ciphers derived from the addition process are referred to as the *Addcap* [the *capstone* from addition]. Mary's Lifepath is a 7, an *addcap*. John's Lifepath is a 9, an *addcap*.

For both of these individuals, the 3 Challenge indicates they will each confront issues and concerns during their lives with some [but not necessarily all] of the attributes associated with the Three energy: self-expression, image, words, art, communication, joy, friends, pleasure, children, health and beauty.

What's your Lifepath Challenge? What is the LP Challenge of your loved ones? Family? Friends? Business partners? To discover the Lifepath Challenge, simply add the numbers of the Lifepath and if there is a binary root [in most cases there will be one], subtract the ciphers to derive the single number, the Subcap, which will be the Challenge and then cross-reference this number with the *Keywords Catalogue* [page 217] to assess the meaning.

Chapter Three

THE EXPRESSION
[Birth Name]

The Expression plays a major role in the love connection. It is derived from our full name at birth. Unlike the Lifepath [our life script], the Expression *is* us, the embodiment of all our assets and liabilities, the actor or actress who reads the life script. It is through our birth name that we *express* ourselves. It is also the full name at birth that sets the destiny. We may acquire other names in our lives such as a married name, a religious confirmation name or a name change for publicity, theatrical or artistic reasons, but the name at birth is the dominant indicator of destiny as far as names are concerned. On very rare occasions a name change will have an effect, but the rule is that the original and full name at birth sets the path of our destiny along with the Lifepath itself.

How can this be so, that our names establish our destiny? The answer is that there are divine forces working in our lives that exceed our understanding. Those forces, those powers, establish our life's course. In effect, we do not have a specific destiny because we have a specific name and lifepath, but rather we have a specific name and lifepath because we have a specific destiny to fulfill, a destiny given to us by God.

This fact of fate is taught by every major religion. Even the great scientist, Dr. Albert Einstein states:

> *Everything is determined, the beginning as well as the end by forces over which we have no control. It is determined for the insect as well as for the star. Human beings, vegetables or cosmic dust, we all dance to a mysterious tune, intoned in the distance by an invisible piper.*

This is a phenomenal statement. It is corroborated in the Biblical passage [St. Matthew 10:30]: *The very hairs of your head are all numbered.* The Koran states: *What God writes on your forehead you will become.* A Yiddish proverb proclaims: *If a man is destined to drown, he will drown even in a spoonful of water.* A French proverb acknowledges: *He that is born to be hanged shall never be drowned.* The Granth Sahib, the holy text of Sikhism says: *The Unknowable Lord's pen inscribes the destinies of all beings on their foreheads.* The famous German dramatist, Johann Friedrich Von Schiller exclaims: *There is no such thing as chance, and what seems to us merest accident springs from the deepest source of destiny.* The great English statesman and leader, Sir Winston Churchill exhorts: *Destiny commands. We must obey!* The Twentieth Century mystic, Charan Singh teaches: *All men come into this world with a destiny of their own which goes on pushing them relentlessly on the course already marked out for them.* And so it goes - on and on and on. Each of our lives is destined, and that destiny is contained in our Expression and Lifepath.

Our Expression contains many secrets regarding who we are and what our destiny holds for us. However, for the purpose of this book, we'll keep things very simple. If the reader would like more information on the Expression, Lifepath or one's destiny, please refer to *The King's Book of Numerology, Volume I: Foundations & Fundamentals* [denoted in short as: KBN I] and *The King's Book of Numerology II: Forecasting - Part I* [denoted as KBN II].

Calculating the Expression

Calculating the Expression is just as simple as calculating the Lifepath. All we're going to do is add some simple numbers together and reduce them to a single digit. First, however, we have to translate the letters of the name into numbers. Use the full name at birth. Some people have just two names, some three or more.

The "Simple Letter Value Chart" below shows the value of each letter in the alphabet. For birth names in other languages simply translate them into English. To find the number associated with the name, follow the three simple steps beneath the chart. Examples follow.

\	Simple Letter Value Chart							
The Letters	A	B	C	D	E	F	G	H	I
	J	K	L	M	N	O	P	Q	R
	S	T	U	V	W	X	Y	Z	
Number Value	1	2	3	4	5	6	7	8	9

1. Write the name down on a piece of paper.
2. Place the number associated with each letter under it.
3. Add the numbers from left to right and reduce to a single digit.

Example #1: Mary Jane Smith

Version A. Full Name

This is the simplest method. Using the "Simple Letter Value Chart" above, add all the letters of the full name together and reduce to a single digit.

M	A	R	Y	J	A	N	E	S	M	I	T	H		
4+	1+	9+	7+	1+	1+	5+	5+	1+	4+	9+	2+	8+	=	57
57 > 5 + 7 = 12 > 1 + 2 = 3															
The Expression of Mary Jane Smith is a **3**															

Version B. Separate Names

This method allows us to see the separate value of each name. After each name is reduced, simply add the values of each name together. The final value will be the same as Version A.

M	A	R	Y			
4+	1+	9+	7+	=	21 > 2 + 1 = 3	Mary is a 3

J	A	N	E			
1+	1+	5+	5+	=	12 > 1 + 2 = 3	Jane is a 3

S	M	I	T	H		
1+	4+	9+	2+	8+	24 > 2 + 4 = 6	Smith is a 6

[Mary] 3 + [Jane] 3 + [Smith] 6 = 12 > 1 + 2 = 3

Example #2: John David Doey

Version A. Full Name

J	O	H	N	D	A	V	I	D	D	O	E	Y		
1+	6+	8+	5+	4+	1+	4+	9+	4+	4+	6+	5+	7+	=	64
64 > 6 + 4 = 10 > 1 + 0 = 1															
The Expression of John David Doey is a **1**															

Version B. Separate Names

J	O	H	N			
1+	6+	8+	5+	=	20 > 2 + 0 = 2	John is a 2

D	A	V	I	D			
4+	1+	4+	9+	4+	=	22 > 2 + 2 = 4	David is a 4

D	O	E	Y			
4+	6+	5+	7+	=	22 > 2 + 2 = 4	Doey is a 4

[John] 2 + [David] 4 + [Doey] 4 = 10 > 1 + 0 = 1

Your turn. What is your Expression or that of someone you love? Grab some paper and a pencil. Here's an expanded grid guide, although you may need more spaces for a longer name.

The Expression of _____ is a ____

Now let's take a look at the general meaning of each number.

Expression Descriptions

The 1 Expression

As a person reflecting a One Expression, you definitely are an individual, your own person. You like to do things your way. You like to lead, not follow. In the family you may be a dominant patriarch or matriarch. In business or commerce, you need to be out front as the boss, manager or employer. You may also be the pioneer, following the beat of your own drum, exploring areas, ideas and concepts unknown to the rest of the masses. You have ideas and can generate them, for you are ruled by the element fire which is always active, alive, vibrant, warming. You are unique, and there is great potential for you to be especially creative with your mind and with words. You are a doer, an activator and initiator, one who gets the ball rolling and the project underway. You do like to be out front, in the lead where all can follow you or be in the center where you are the focus of attention. You do not like to share the spotlight as a general rule. You may well be an entrepreneur in the commercial/business arena.

In the One Expression there is great emphasis on the self, your self. This is fine if you do not allow the dominant, powerful, creative, vibrant One energy to become too self-absorbed and individually all-consuming. The highest expression of the One is union with the Divine. The lowest expression is negative egomania where one feels the entire world and universe revolve around him or her - a totally self-centered, self-consumed, self-absorbed, arrogant, imperious, egomaniacal, overbearing, unbending dictator. To keep the One humble, it must be remembered that there is only one true One and that is God from whom all the other little ones originate, and He may, at His slightest whim, expunge any little one who is not reflecting the majesty, truth, grandeur, creativity and oneness of His One.

Therefore, as a One Expression, there is great responsibility on your shoulders. You can reflect the majesty of His Oneness through a process of merging with Him, or you can reflect the distasteful arrogance of the little one trying to be a big-shot. The latter would be a result of separation, not union, with the Divine. But One is Union, not separation, so the only feasible solution is to deny the little ego by acknowledging the only Ego - His Ego, His Presence. A One Expression may live life, therefore, as the drop of water separate from the ocean or as the drop which has merged with the ocean, thereby, reflecting its power and beauty.

On a more mundane note, Ones have strong wills. This is important from a leadership position. As a leader, One must take a stand and lead, not bend and break or worse, descend into the flock where confusion and chaos will possibly reign if there is no leadership, if there is no one with the strength, conviction, wherewithal and basic guts to stand up and say, "Follow me!" Leadership is always a lonely, frightening, uncomfortable, solitary experience because the leader is out front for all to see, acclaim or defame. However, it's easy to criticize from the pack, especially if the burden of leadership is on someone else's shoulders. Being a leader means making tough decisions and having the courage to stick by them. Leadership is additionally difficult because it is impossible to please all the people all the time. It's a rough and tough job but society must have leaders and this is one of the potential roles for the person who reflects the One Expression.

As a leader, the fundamental precept to follow is simply to act on the principle of Oneness. We are all part of a whole, one united Being with multiple hands and feet. A man may be an island, but nobody is a world. We all exist together on one planet, one shrinking planet, where, eventually, everyone must learn to act as one, not two, if for no other reason than basic global survival. We are, indeed, one world. The true leader is the one who sees this and creates oneness, not separateness; who creates union, not disunion.

The strength of will of the One Expression becomes negative when the one becomes so rigid it does not bend. However, One must bend at times, just not break. Take, for example, the solitary and beautiful willow tree. It stands strong and alone but its branches bend to accommodate the wind. In other words, it gives in where it has to. This does not diminish it, for the tree sustains no damage from the wind. Its inherent structure simply allows it to bend and survive.

Another aspect of the One Expression is the self. Self is an important concept but, once again, the self has two sides: one positive; one negative. The positive self is the one 'at one' with its Source. The negative one is the one separate from its Source and acting independently. This may seem enigmatic but it is not. In the realm of separate entities, as all of us are in the worldly scheme of things, we naturally possess a unique individuality. But we are nothing without a common Source uniting us all. To illustrate this we can simply see each of us as a separate light bulb - unique, separate, individual - but, nonetheless, a bulb like every other bulb which receives its brilliance from one source - the electric current. Without the current, each bulb, each of us, is lightless and lifeless. Yes, we are individuals but we all run on the same current and derive our life energy from the same Source.

Another example is that we are all bubbles floating on the surface of the ocean. Yes, we are separate but not dis-separate from our Source, once again. Furthermore, as a bubble our life span is not very long. Thus, why get too involved with our fleeting individuality which is temporal? It is best, therefore, to identify with the one Current which gives us life, to identify with the vast Ocean of the Spirit from which we gain our true identity, our true self.

The One Expression is a masculine energy. Does this mean that a female maintaining a One Expression is not feminine? No. Quite the contrary. It simply means that she will tend to be more logical and reasonable than she might otherwise be, as logic and reason are male/yang characteristics. She will, as a One Expression, naturally possess energies of leadership, creation, initiation and action. She will be self-motivated, will take charge and get things done without being told to if she is in a support role as a secretary, assistant or helper of some kind. If she is in a prime leadership role as a manager, president or executive, she has the inherent ability to lead exceptionally well by infusing her One Expression male/yang energy with her inherent Two female/yin energy. Male One Expression leaders run the risk of being too overbearing and dominant because of their natural concentration of One energy. A female, on the other hand, can balance the male yang energy of leadership with her intrinsic female yin energy of support, caring, nurturing and compassion. She must simply avoid being too vacillating, which is a female/yin characteristic. Leaders of any sex may change their minds, but they cannot be vacillatory nor illogical or overly emotional if they choose to be effective leaders. Leadership requires action and courage and the best of all leadership is that which is balanced by both male and female energies.

As a One Expression, enjoy your uniqueness, for you are unique and original. Enjoy your independence. Enjoy your creative abilities. Be excited by your ability to take action and to lead. Not everyone can act, create, generate, initiate and lead as you do. But do not look down on others because they are not leaders or because they cannot create or take action. That's your job. A leader needs followers; followers need leaders. Neither is more important than the other. It's all part of the whole polarity scene of this creation. Be wary of becoming too self-centered. It is best to be divinely Self-Centered, i.e., acknowledging God as the only True One, which He obviously is.

The 2 Expression

As a person reflecting a Two Expression, you are one who supports, helps, cares for and sustains others. You have compassion, kindness and a gentleness of manner. Your passive nature allows you to be unobtrusive, soft, friendly, congenial, agreeable, cordial, conciliatory, cooperative and comprising. Because you are ruled by the Two, you can generally see both sides of an issue and often serve as a peacemaker or diplomat. Your emotional energy brings feelings to situations where pure logic and reason are found lacking. You tend to be intuitive and receptive, flowing and working with situations rather than attempting to impose your will and ego on others. You are considered the peacemaker of the Alpha-Numeric Spectrum.

The Two Expression is governed by the female yin energy of the universe. You are a follower by nature, giving those dominated by One energy a chance to lead and experience the lesson of the self. You tend to be subordinate and possibly submissive but this does not make you less important in the least. After all, cosmic, universal structure is comprised of two distinct energies - the One and the Two, the yang and the yin. Neither is more important than the other. They both comprise the whole. But they do have different qualities and characteristics - in fact, opposite and oftentimes contrapuntal, if not contentious by their very nature.

The Two Expression is centered in relationships. This is why women, and men with a Two Expression or other Two energy in their charts, are more in tune with relationships than men in general or women dominated by a strong One influence. Females are ruled by this number Two energy of relationships whereas males, who are ruled by the number One, live in the world of ideas and action. Women live in the world of others and reaction. One is day. Two is night. Both are ends of the same continuum. Both are critical to the cosmic structure. However, neither men or women are purely yang (male) or yin (female). Both sexes are a blend of One and Two energy, although One energy is generally associated with men and Two energy with women.

The Two energy is powerful in its ability to support. This is why women have often been characterized as the "power behind the throne," especially in the past. But all that is changing. Women are now moving to the forefront of society and becoming the "power on the throne."

An interesting cosmic note is that, from a numerological perspective, our earth has entered the Second Millennium. This means that the Two energy will be highlighted for a thousand years. Thus, a person with a Two Expression will feel more comfortable in this millennium than in the First Millennium where the number One dominated. The cosmic pendulum has now swung the other way. We have experienced a thousand years of the One male energy of the yang and it is now time for the earth to experience the Two female energy of the yin - a very opposite polarity with opposite attributes and characteristics.

This polar shift is one of the main reasons we see such confusion in our world today. All of us alive at this time, particularly those born before the year 2000, or who have parents or friends who were, are experiencing, either directly or indirectly, both of these contrasting polar vibrations of the One and Two! As explained in *The Age of the Female: A Thousand Years of Yin* [available at www.richardking.net], those souls born after the year 2031 will only know the polar vibration of the Two. Hence, they will not know by direct experience the vibration of the One except vicariously through the eyes and tongues of those of us who were born in the nineteen hundreds. Thus, they will not have the understanding of having lived in both yang and yin vibratory periods. That gift, if it can be called that, is reserved only for those who have lived in the Twentieth and Twenty-First centuries, quite a distinction when one thinks about it. What other souls in creation can claim this unique experience?

A Two Expression person will obviously harmonize with the Second Millennium. As the Two Expression is focused in the realm of 'others', so the Second Millennium will be one of 'others' as well. This will not be a time glorifying the sovereignty of isolated and separate nations and people. This will be a time of learning to get along with others, to share our world, to be concerned about what others do in the scheme of world balance, health and equilibrium. Relationships will be important, relationships that engender peace and harmony.

One of the cautions of the Two Expression rests in its quality of duality. At its spiritual zenith, Two rules balance, peace, compassion, equilibrium and harmony. However, at its negative nadir, it is a vibration of opposition, competition, contention, conflict, imbalance, hostility, antagonism, disunity, separation, argumentation and friction. The number Two can be viewed as the analogy of the tug-o-war with both sides, both polar extremes, pulling equally from both directions. The Two can also be viewed as the teeter-totter in constant imbalance, rising and falling in almost perpetual motion. This is why the Two is viewed as emotional - it lacks one continuous motion, thus reflecting a state of "e-motion" - being out of motion.

Thus, as a Two Expression, you must guard against this polarization creating imbalance, inharmony and contention. You have the ability to generate great peace, harmony, kindness and compassion, but like all vibrations, the Two also has its opposite side, and the opposite of harmony is inharmony; the opposite of balance is imbalance; the opposite of peace is war.

One unites. Two separates and divides. In our society today we probably have more separate and distinct factions than at any other time in world history, and the number seems to be growing. Under the Two vibration, people divide into groups and take sides. These sides oppose each other and will oppose each other until everyone learns that harmonious life is the result of balance, the positive aspect of the Two, not destructive opposition, its negative aspect.

The beauty of the Two lies in expressing unity, not disunity. This is the challenge of the Second Millennium. It is also the challenge of the Two Expression. Make peace, not war. Create harmony, not disharmony. Think of others, not of self. Respect those who support and serve, not just those who lead while being maintained by the support of others. Cooperate; don't dominate. Compromise. Find the Golden Mean, the middle ground between polarities. Create peace. This is the great calling for the Two Expression.

For more information on the number Two and its dominance of the current thousand years, read *The Age of the Female: A Thousand Years of Yin* and *The Age of the Female II: Heroines of the Shift* available at richardking.net.

The 3 Expression

As a Three Expression you are definitely expressive. You are pleasant to be around. You smile a great deal of the time. You are friendly, easy to know, and emit a positive attitude. Generally, you like to talk, visit with friends, socialize. Words may be an important part of who you are. You may like to write, especially if you also maintain some dominant Seven energy in your chart. You are most probably very attractive and there is an excellent chance you will be associated with the arts in some capacity - this to fulfill your personal sense of self-expression and communication. If your personal Expression is elevated to the nineties decade with a 93 root, you may well want to express yourself on the public stage of life or, perhaps, even in the theater as an actor or actress. If your General Expression is rooted in the eighties decade with an 84 root, your Three Expression will most likely be manifested in the world of business and commerce. If your Three has a sixty-six root, you may well love to sing or use your voice to bring love and harmony to others. You may also be driven to write, to express your thoughts and deepest feelings on paper as a journalist, playwright, sports writer, composer, fiction or non-fiction author. Your mental skill with words could also propel you into the television milieu as a commentator, news-anchor, reporter, host or announcer. As a Three Expression, communication in some capacity is vital to your being. For more information regarding the Expression and its root structures, read *The King's Book of Numerology, Volume I: Foundations & Fundamentals).*

The key word to describe you though is certainly self-expression. Even if you do not use words as much as other Threes, you may find yourself visually expressing and communicating your talent in the health and beauty field, perhaps as a model, beautician, make-up artist, clothes designer, etc. How you integrate your body, mind and spirit is important to you, for the Three is the cosmic vibration which completes the male-female, positive-negative polar connection. This is reflected in the symbol of the triangle which is the ancient symbol for perfection. In the triangle we can see the balance of the One and Two energy being brought together to create a completed circuit. When this cosmic circuit is completed, balance between the opposing polarities is created and one becomes happy, fulfilled and expressive as a natural extension of a balanced condition. Where there is balance, there is peace and ease, no contention, friction or stress generated as a result of opposing polarities pulling and tugging on each other.

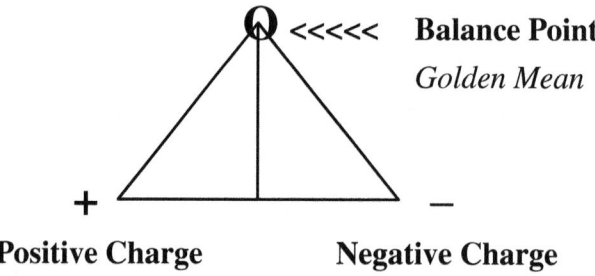

This balanced state is the reason the Three vibration is seen as that basic vibration generating the most ease of the nine major energy fields. As a Three Expression, you are a person who generates this ease, comfort, like-ability, friendliness and fun.

The number Three is also the number of the Trinity: Father, Son and Holy Ghost; Master, Disciple and Word. Therefore, an individual with a divinely elevated sense of this cosmic vibration may well be involved spiritually or religiously, expressing the divine connection and integration which is intrinsic to the Three vibration. In fact, this aspect of the Three is the reflection of its greatest meaning - divine integration of the body, mind and spirit which moves and ascends upward toward the Divine apex.

Since all vibrations have their negative side, as certainly as the Three can bring integration, ease, health and beauty, it can also bring disintegration, dis-ease, sickness and ugliness of one sort or another. Negative self-expression, self-harm, self-mutilation or self-destruction are possible with a negatively aspected Three, as well as being unlikable in a social sense. What can be perfect can also be imperfect. Beauty, like sickness, does not last forever. Happiness, in a worldly context, is as ephemeral as sadness. Remember, the cosmic pendulum swings both ways, and where there is health, there is also the potential of disease or dis-ease.

In consideration of this cosmic fact, when we have or reflect enjoyment, ease, comfort, beauty and friends, we must not forget the spiritual purpose of life - that of God-Realization. Too often when situations, conditions, times, or our personal self-expression, are good, pleasant, enjoyable and fulfilling, we forget our Divine Roots, much to our eventual chagrin. We can be thrown off the mark, off the balance beam, just as easily by joy as by tragedy. Balance, represented by the Golden Mean [the middle ground of the triangle], should not be forgotten. Rather, it should be the focus of the Three energy, for ultimately the Three Expression is about personal expression through Divine Integration, not wanton and excessive self-indulgent gratification and pleasure.

There are three cautions with the Three Expression. The first is excessive vanity. The number Three rules image, and if one's personal image is not controlled it will expand to destructive degrees. It is important to have a healthy self-image, no doubt, but when carried to extremes that image becomes very distasteful.

A second caution is entitlement. Three rules ease of living, comfort, joy and good fortune. Such things are wonderful blessings, but they should not be taken for granted or expected. Sometimes having too much of a good thing can be a curse as much as a blessing. Such good fortune should not be flaunted or imposed upon others with thoughtless disregard and egocentric abandon. We do reap what we sow, and sowing entitlement and ingratitude will result in good fortune being taken away.

A third caution is over-indulgence in pleasure. Three rules pleasure of all kinds, but when that pleasure is focused too much in the material world, the results will be painfully tragic. Over-indulgence in alcohol, drugs, sex and personal power is the harbinger of a great fall. Numerology archives are filled with cases of individuals whose lives were destroyed because of unchecked wanton self-indulgence. Societies have collapsed because of the same situation. Certainly, Rome had its issues with over-indulgence in its higher echelons of society which contributed to its downfall. For an individual desirous of a contented life, it must be remembered that the flip side of pleasure is pain, and the more pleasure is sought for, the more pain will be experienced. As Saint Charan Singh has stated: *No matter how great the pleasures of the world may be, they are not only short lived but also have equally unpleasant reactions at some time or another.* Therefore, as has been mentioned repeatedly, balance is primary in all things.

As a positively charged Three Expression, it's important to share your sense of joy and happiness with others. A smile, a laugh, a good word, a sincere ear and a few light-hearted moments go a long way in easing other people's worries. Your joy is infectious. Let it shine.

Too, be the artist you intrinsically are. Write, sing, paint, debate, sculpt, act, compose, model. Let the joyous strings, pipes, drums and ivory keys of your basic nature fill other people with your positive energy. You are an artist after all, a communicator, a bringer of joy, hope and happiness. We all need you, especially in a world where joy and happiness are such rare commodities.

The 4 Expression

The Four Expression is the rock and salt of the earth. Four is the vibration representing the structures of our lives - physically, mentally, emotionally, socially, maritally, financially. If your Four Expression is not negatively aspected in your chart, you are a solid, dependable, reliable, hard-working, trustworthy, devoted, service-oriented individual who is more rooted than any of the other nine vibrations. You are an anchor, and people depend on you often to anchor them and give them strength. The ultimate expression of the Four energy is one of service, work and effort, moving, sometimes plodding, along with undiminished regularity and dogged persistence.

Your Four Expression may be expressed in the creative field as a painter, sculptor, designer, photographer. The Four energy constructs, especially in the world of form, so your artistic abilities may take shape as great works of tangible or visual art.

The symbol of the Four is the square and represents the foundations and structures of our lives. Depending upon our perspective, we can stand on top of the square, using it as a foundation; be protected and guarded by it by dwelling within the security of its walls, or be crushed by its weight by existing below it. Therefore, how we use our Four energy is vital to our sense of strength and security. All of these locations in relation to the square can give security. However, they can also give a sense of limitation and imprisonment because the Four, unlike the Five, does not move or change. It stays put, rooted in place like the Rock of Gibraltar.

The Three Placements of the Square

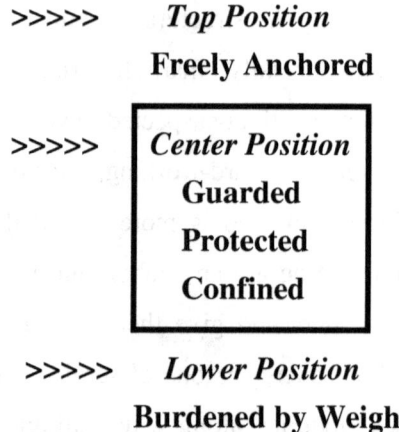

>>>>>   *Top Position*
        Freely Anchored

>>>>>   *Center Position*
        Guarded
        Protected
        Confined

>>>>>   *Lower Position*
        Burdened by Weight

In the Top Position, we are anchored to life but free enough to experience the world around us. In the Center Position, we are confined within the square. Depending upon our make-up, this may be comforting or confining. In the Lower Position, we are burdened by the weight of the Four, perhaps even feeling crushed by the mass of its vibrations. We may even experience all three positions at once or at separate times. The point is that we will feel the weight and gravity of the Four, positively or negatively.

Positive Fours are very secure people; rock solid and oozing with control, dependability, reliability and trust. Negative Fours often violate the principle of structure in their lives and become imprisoned or pressed down by its weight. For example, if a person is not trustworthy, is not reliable, is not dependable, is not faithful, is not disciplined, is not controlled, then only trouble can ensue.

The great vibration of the Four Expression demands structure, control and the purity, persistence, effort and sacrifice of action and behavior characteristic of the long-suffering of Noah and his family during the forty days of rain upon the earth and the forty days of the Flood; of Moses and his people in the desert for forty years, of Moses himself on Mount Sinai for forty days and nights and, of course, Jesus in the wilderness for forty days. Forty, whose crown is the Four, is the vibration representing purification through discipline, determination, self-control, restraint, continence, work, effort, toil, limitation, regimentation, regulation, order, sacrifice and unrelenting persistence. When these qualities are learned and expressed, the result is ultimate strength and security. But make no mistake, there can be no strength and security without the aforementioned virtues. Strength is, itself, a virtue but it can not be manifested without those qualities which comprise its structure and which give it form.

One of the hazards of the Four Expression is being so overly consumed with the principle of 'structure' that one becomes stuck in the mud, unable to move and change when one's best interest may call for some type of adaptation to the structure, maybe even to leave the structure like a snake shedding its skin. Some Fours can be so stubborn and resistant at times they give new meaning to the word 'jack ass'. If, for example, one believes in loyalty, he is under no law to jump off a cliff at the behest of another person, taking his life in the process, however strongly he believes in loyalty. God does not condone suicide under any circumstances. A person, however, who is overly saturated with a misguided sense of devotion and loyalty, may not have the good, common and divine sense to see outside the box and make the proper adjustments and take the proper actions to protect his ultimate divine security. It is good to be rooted but not so immovable that one jeopardizes his health and well-being, or that of others, in the process. Thus, the balanced Four Expression needs to reflect practicality but not be impractical.

You are a Four Expression. Be strong. Be secure. Be stable. Be practical. Be disciplined. Be dependable, reliable, trustworthy, loyal, faithful, devoted. Work hard - there can be no excellence without effort. Live by a code of life, a living structure of rules and regulations. Serve life because you are the great servant. Keep your priorities in line and forever. . . be the rock!

The 5 Expression

As a Five Expression, you are the epitome of motion, movement, change, experience, adventure and versatility. You love your freedom and do not like to be restricted. Unlike the Four Expression which plants roots and seeks a grounded stability, you generally have few roots and prefer stability in motion. Your love of freedom makes you seem unstable at times but stability is a relative concept. An airplane in flight, for example, is not stable in a 'grounded' sense but quite stable in a moving/flying sense. In fact, it needs the movement of the air over its wings to keep it stable. Motion and movement are critical to its balance, health and well-being. Without such motion, the plane would crash and burn. As a Five Expression, you are much like an airplane - motion not only makes you free, it keeps you stable. Therefore, do not worry about those who see you as unstable. You simply have a different functional understanding of stability.

Change is important to you. The movement you need in your life is not simply physical movement, it is psychological, social, vocational, sexual, emotional, and spiritual as well. You thrive on new experiences because they feed your desire to know more, explore more, do more. Change, constant change, is the vehicle through which you acquire this experience. This also makes you talented in many areas. Doing one thing is not enough for you. You need the input of varied stimuli to keep you alive and excited. If you receive this stimulation, your Five energy is complete and you feel satisfied. If there is too little stimulation, you wither and wane. You are not meant to be the rock, confined to one place your whole life. You are meant to be the eagle, to fly, to soar, to be free, to ride the ever-changing winds of life, enthralled with the majesty of motion in flight.

As a Five Expression, you may definitely have many talents and be a person for all people (see *The King's Book of Numerology, Volume I: Foundations & Fundamentals*). You will be a person who loves to socialize with friends, seeking pleasure and good times. You will possibly enjoy exploring things mentally, psychologically and spiritually if you also have Seven energy supporting your Five. There is the distinct possibility your sense of movement in the arena of the heart, romance, the home and family will give you many experiences, adventures and lessons in freedom and detachment.

As a Five Expression, you must guard against over indulgence in sensual pleasures of all kinds. The Five loves to experience and explore but some things are better left unexplored and unexperienced. Who, in their right mind, would ever want to be sucked into the dark abyss of a black hole? Yet, there are many black holes in this world. Not all experiences or adventures are positive, let alone spiritual, and many experiences lead to incarceration, not freedom. Alcohol, drugs and illicit sexuality are black holes to the soul. Free indulgence in them leads to imprisonment in the world of the senses from which escape is extremely difficult. In effect, nothing is free. Everything has a price. Never forget that. In spite of contemporary thought and wishful thinking, there is no such thing as free love, free drinks, free anything. We must simply, and truthfully, pay for everything we get in life. Neglecting spiritual law and its edict of discipline, self-control and temperance leads to imprisonment, and imprisonment is not a pleasant, comfortable or enjoyable experience. If the Five is not careful, it will rue the day it sought too much experience after demanding too much freedom and over-indulging its sensual appetite when it should have exercised more discipline and restraint. As Pythagoras said, *No man is free who cannot control himself.* More than any other number, the Five needs to heed this lesson.

Therefore, for the Five Expression, discretion and a positive sense of discrimination - the ability to discern what is healthful or harmful, is critical for this freedom-loving, experiencing-seeking explorer and adventurer. Learning to make right choices to advance one's spiritual evolution is more important than simply making a choice to be free and adventurous. If we can progress in our life's journey, we can regress as well. Where we go and where we will be tomorrow depends upon the choices we make today, now, in the present, for as certain as the sun shines, there will be consequences to our every action and we will have to pay the price for the things and experiences we choose to buy and bear.

The Five vibration must be seen and understood correctly from a spiritual perspective. The Five loves freedom but true freedom is based on and is the product of extreme discipline, regulation, restriction and self-control. Unrestrained, unregulated, undisciplined action does not create freedom because all actions have their consequences, and the consequence of unrestrained behavior is captivity and destruction. Freedom is not "license carte blanche." Freedom is action taken in consideration of consequence.

As a Five Expression, you must carry this truth with you throughout your life, for the choices you make today will determine where you are tomorrow. The Five offers great freedom of choice but its inherent danger is that those choices could send you just as easily to heaven as to hell. Freedom is wonderful, but the abuse of freedom will send the soul into the darkest and most horror-filled dungeons imaginable. Therefore, use discretion, discrimination and foresight in making every choice at every step along the path of your life. Look ahead at the possible consequences to your actions *before* you take them. And remember, those choices promising fulfillment and satiation of and by the senses, although pleasurable and easy to make, often take the soul down a nether road to a dark and sorrow-filled land where freedom, even as a word, doesn't exist.

Fives must be careful also of becoming too scattered and too free, just as the Four must be careful of becoming too stable, too rooted. Balance is the key in all things. Because the Five moves at breakneck speed, it must be careful it doesn't fall and break its own neck. It is not uncommon for Fives to be accident-prone because they are doing so much so quickly they forget to concentrate on the task at hand. It's fine to move fast but one cannot afford to lose his concentration, just as a race car driver cannot afford to lose his. And Fives do like speed. Fast cars, fast horses, fast boats, fast planes, fast feet, fast intentions and fast experiences are part of the Five energy.

As a Five Expression, you are very personable. You like talking and visiting with others and can be extremely animated, charismatic, charming and dashing. Therefore, you would do well in fields involving the public and/or where you could move freely with little restriction. A nine-to-five job sitting in some back room or cubicle is not for you. Leave that to the Fours. You need a job in which you can be free to move about experiencing and sharing your talents with others. This does not mean you are irresponsible. Irresponsibility has nothing to do with freedom. It has to do with personal integrity. You can be as responsible as any other person. Nor does it mean you should lead a wanton, sensually-driven, libidinously saturated life in violation of spiritual law. You just cannot be constricted or restricted if you are to do your best work and be at your optimum health.

As a Five Expression, be free. Move. Fly. Change. It's okay to change. Experience. Explore. Enjoy your enthusiasm and let others enjoy it as well, but know the difference between true freedom and freedom carte blanche. Bad choices made under the superficial pretense of freedom can be painfully binding and bonding, relegating you, not to fields of freedom but to dungeons of bondage. True freedom, after all, detaches us from the world of form and phenomena, liberating us from this dimension of delusion and lifting us to higher skies where our spirit is unequivocally free of all dross and gross material trappings.

The 6 Expression

As a Six Expression, your entire being revolves around and is centered in your heart. Love of family, romance and close friends is extremely important to you. On a social level, you may well have a concern for the community as well. There is a softness about you, a gentleness which makes you the nurturer, the one who gives to others, embraces and supports them, keeping them warm and secure. If you are a female, you are the Mother of the Earth. If you are a male, you are the caring, compassionate patriarch. You enjoy beauty and harmony. Always, your heart remains at home.

As a Six Expression, you most likely are a lover of beauty. Six is a higher octave of two (the vibration of balance) and of three (the energy of beauty and integrated perfection). Six, therefore, is an amalgamation of these energies, expressing beauty, balance, creativity, harmony and sweetness.

As a Six, you most probably enjoy music very much and may even be an exquisite and exceptionally expressive performer. You may love to sing, creating beauty and harmony with your voice and words, soothing the tensions of others as well as yourself. Many great singers and performers have Six dominant in their numerology charts.

There is no doubt the home and domestic environment are intrinsically important to you. Devotion and loyalty are key. Six rules the home, heart and hearth and no other vibration is as attached or focused upon the domestic scene as you are. Trust your sense of being the loving parent and know that eight/ninths of the world does not have what you possess - a love of home and everything and everyone in it.

One of the attributes associated with the Six vibration is adjustment. Personal lives change, and as the lives of our loved ones change, as they will, the Six must adjust to keep everything in the home and heart balanced.

One red flag for the Six Expression is that while Six is the vibration of pure, personal, nurturing love, the opposite side of the coin is hate and its affiliate attributes of jealousy, envy, bitterness.

Love and hate are the positive and negative warp and woof of the tapestry of the Six vibration. In this dimension where one occurs, the other must also be present. This is why people in love often hurt, even kill, their lovers. Certainly, to walk the line of worldly love is to walk the razor's edge. Passion is passion and, although it can bring pleasure, it can also be manifested as displeasure in varying degrees. As a positive aside, just remember that people who hate you actually love you because their minds are always filled with you. They are absorbed with you, even though their thoughts and feelings may not be pleasant to us. When we hold a coin, we hold both sides simultaneously, so when the coin of love is in our hands, its flip side, hate, is also in our grasp. Another thing to remember is that the energy of hate is more destructive to the hater, the person who creates and holds the hate, than to anyone else. Hate is an extremely negative energy and is the cause of not only excessive dis-ease, but a myriad of diseases. As Saint Dariya of Bihar states: *The sower of the poison cannot but be engulfed in the poison.* And as Saint Ravidas confirms: *The fruit of action unfailingly overtakes the doer.* Excellent food for thought.

Six rules love. One expression of worldly love is lust, i.e. sexual gratification. Since Six is two times three and Three is the energy of pleasure, another red flag emerges. If one's romantic passions are not held in check, trouble can and often does arise with the Six Expression. It can even be far greater than that caused by the Three's misuse. Loving relationships, not lusting relationships, demand responsibility to both parties. However, one's passion for sexual gratification may often override one's loyalty to his or her significant other, the family and the community, bringing a wave of negative feedback, pain, sorrow, destruction and tears in the process. This is where the responsibility and devotion factors of the Six must come into play. Where there is responsibility, there is balance and beauty. Where there is irresponsibility, there is imbalance and ugliness.

It is, therefore, important to separate love from lust, love from passion. While many people say they are in love, they are really only expressing their passion, their carnal desires, their lust. Love, true love, elevates the soul. Passion (lust) debases the soul. Love purifies. Lust adulterates. Love always upgrades while lust degrades. Love cares about the highest and best good of those upon whom it is focused. Lust only cares for itself. Love would never jeopardize the health and well-being of another. Lust could care less for another's welfare.

Why is this important? Because Six Expression individuals have the ability to bring true personal love into manifestation. They can be the great mothers, the great fathers, the great nurturers of mankind; the true, devoted and loyal lovers who embrace the love of all in their hearts. Or. . . they can be the depraved and wanton libertines who use others to satisfy their own carnal and depraved appetites. As the Five Expression walks the road between freedom and slavery, the Six Expression walks the road between love and hate. We all have choices at every step, and those choices will determine our future. Such choices will also determine the love or hate we will receive in future lifetimes, as the Great Law of Karma is always operating in this dimension, returning to the doer the actions of his/hers deeds.

The 7 Expression

Seven Expression people are the most misunderstood of the nine basic expressions. They often seem aloof, cold, unconcerned, distant, untouchable. Yet, although they may be aloof from the wishes and whims of an externally-based society, they are potentially extremely deep and in touch with the depths of their psyches. "Still waters run deep", and Sevens are deep. They are the thinkers of society, the ones who ponder, reflect, analyze, scrutinize. They do not care to be connected to the outer world because their connections are with the inner world. They know things others do not know or cannot know for they are deeply connected to the Force within.

This depth is manifested in their spiritual, religious, metaphysical behavior. It isn't that there is anything wrong with the outside world, it's just not their world. Their world is much more private, reclusive and isolated. Their need is to be alone and separate from others; to think, meditate, ponder, cogitate and reflect. Because most of the world is socially oriented, it does not understand Sevens and their need to be alone. But Sevens do understand themselves and that is all that is necessary. This separation from others appears to them that Sevens are cold, aloof and distant but Seven individuals are not cold, distant or aloof from the fiery spirit permeating their every pore. There is a reality within Seven individuals that those who live on the outside simply cannot understand nor appreciate. Therefore, Sevens create their own private space to pursue their interests and find their own peace.

These deep connections do not come without a price. That price is often the censure, criticism, ridicule and ostracism of others. Therefore, Sevens must be calm and serene to balance this unknowing of others and their possible untoward behavior toward them. They can't help themselves. They are just not deeply connected enough to understand how deep Seven people really are, how unconcerned they are with the external world and its superficial existence.

Thus, the Seven Expression person often finds himself alone. This state of isolation, and perhaps alienation, can be painful because even though he is deeply connected, he is still human and although he does not require the same external contact that others crave, it is difficult to be an isolated island within the stream of humanity. We all need contact with others and we have an intrinsic need to touch and be touched - not necessarily physically but emotionally and mentally. And here is where the Seven's special vibratory pattern shines. Because of its inward-dwelling sense of life, it has the ability to make the internal connection which those living in the external world cannot make. So the admonition of Seven people is, "do it." Make the internal, eternal connection. When this connection is made, there will be no more isolation because there will only be oneness, Oneness with God, the Creator of All that ever was, that is or will ever be. There is no connection greater than this and there is no connection giving such peace and everlasting bliss. Those who desire this divine peace must also travel the way of the Seven, for Seven is the key to the inner regions, to the Royal Realm where God resides.

Seven loves to have its space, and no number needs its own space more than the Seven. Others in its world need to know this so they can make the proper adjustments and keep the relationship harmonious. It is not that the Seven is not connected to others, it's just not connected to others in an external sense. Its depth of knowing can be a great anchor in other people's ocean of turmoil.

Seven is the vibration of supreme peace. Its opposite polarity is the vibration of supreme chaos. The Seven may be exhibiting one or the other polarity but the end to which it must aspire for its spiritual ascendancy is, of course, peace. This means it is necessary to stay centered in the eye of the hurricane where all is still and calm.

Pythagoras, the father of numerology, said Seven is the most sacred of all numbers because it's a synthesis of the trine of the spirit [ruled by the number Three] and the square of matter [ruled by the number Four]. Other world religions corroborate this fact of the Seven's sanctity which is the most mentioned number in the Bible, especially in the Book of Revelation. In fact, the 3-4-7 triad is the most mentioned set of numbers in the Bible. Thus, a Seven Expression person is saturated with the potential of spirituality.

Carrying this further, it is worthy of note that one of the two numbers most often prevalent in the charts of substantively famous people whose reputations have stood the test of time is the number Seven. This is because Seven rules the spirit and it is the Spirit that every living soul has in common by divine decree. The Seven energy sensitizes us and makes us feel deeply, connecting with others in a way that is impossible for any other number. The other number prevalent in the charts of famous people is the Nine, the energy of universality, without whose energies it is difficult to obtain recognition and notoriety on the public stage.

Seven is not only the most potentially spiritual of all the numbers, it is also the most secretive and private. Sevens will always seek some degree of privacy. If they can't get it, they will create it by possibly starting a confrontation which they can use as a reason for some temporary separation. It's critical that people associated with a Seven person understand that the Seven person needs time alone because it's in their isolation that the Seven recharges and re-centers itself.

As far as secrecy goes, the Seven individual should be judicious and discerning. Some things are best left private, but secrecy can also create suspicion and have a negative effect on relationships. The foundation of all relationships is trust, and if the trust between people is destroyed because of secretive and untoward behaviors, the relationship may well be destroyed too.

Seven people can be very anal, i.e., overly meticulous. This is good for jobs requiring exactness and perfection. The problem arises when other people are not as meticulous and perceive the Seven person as being critical. Therefore, Sevens need to be cautious when dispensing help to others, and if they have to offer positive criticism to do so with warmth and tenderness.

The Seven is a very special number. It is intrinsically different from the other numbers in the alpha-numeric spectrum. Its goal is to be patient, appreciate its love of isolation and separation, seek perfection softly and go within where it is most at home and at peace.

The 8 Expression

As a positive Eight Expression, you are a person who loves to connect, interact and integrate. You are success-oriented, generally social by design, love money, wealth, status, power, position and social prominence. You can lead and manage well. You are not reclusive and introspective like the Seven, but outwardly driven, seeking to make yourself a worldly success. You can also work hard and efficiently, seeing what needs to be done and doing it. You are not just a worker. You are the one who orchestrates and coordinates the work, making things run smoothly - like a well-oiled machine. If you are an athlete, you are, no doubt, very coordinated and most likely the tops in your sport. As a performer, you know how to connect with your audience and with your subject matter. You are quite skilled at interacting with others, which gives you a powerful social presence. You mix well with just about everyone. Success is vital to your well-being.

In many cases the Eight Expression will function smoothly in the world of business and commerce, focusing its energies in the fields of management, marketing, sales, advertising and finance.

The Eight Expression wants to integrate, connect and interact. As the highest octave of the 2-4-6-8 quartet, it is socially focused and likes to be involved in the external, worldly, social loop of success, wealth, riches, fame, name and power.

This interconnective attribute is expressed in the ancient lemniscate, the symbolic figure Eight representative of connection and 'flow' between the polar extremes of positive and negative charges. The lemniscate represents the cosmic energy loop connecting opposite polarities: male/female; buyer/seller, idea/manifestation, product/market, etc. A smooth flow is well-coordinated and efficient. When polar charges are brought together, there is success, a normal attribute of the Eight energy. It is the Eight Expression which reflects the function of this ancient symbol more than any other number. Eights love to be on the move, flowing in the loop of success, making the connections needed to realize and manifest their desires and goals. Whether it's the loop of business, the loop of high society, the loop of the artistic world in its many varied forms, the loop of government - the Eight Expression is there. The energy flow of the loop is its lifeblood.

The Lemniscate Eight Loop

Positive Pole [+]   [-] Negative Pole

However, not everything connects under the Eight vibration. As things can connect, they can disconnect as well. This disconnection characteristic is the natural opposing polarity of the connective attribute of the Eight. As we recall, all numbers have a positive and negative charge within themselves. The negative disconnective aspect of the Eight is why people under this vibration can be just as disconnective in their personalities and behavior as those who are quite noticeably connective and successful.

Success and failure are opposing poles of the same continuum, opposite sides of the same coin, opposite ends of the teeter-totter. Therefore, the Eight Expression may create success - actions which connect, integrate and interact, as well as create failure - actions which disconnect, disintegrate and are non-interactive, if not inhibitive and even destructive. This explains why some people under the Eight are successful with money, personal relationships and financial management and others are not. In the latter case, such inefficient use of money and an inability to maintain relationships may be exacerbated by a lack of Hs, Qs and Zs in the natal name (the Expression). These letters carry an Eight value numerologically and a lack of them oftentimes manifests as difficulty in the process of making and maintaining connections and integrating the flow of energy between polar extremes or between people in general. Many single people are often found missing Eights because this is the vibration which connects, and where there is no energy of connection, there is disconnection or inhibition.

Another concern with the Eight lies in the concept of negative manipulation. Because Eight seeks to connect and be successful, it may tend to do so at the expense of moral and ethical behavior, manipulating everything and everybody to get what it wants. The worldly lure of power, wealth, riches, fame, name and success, which fuels the engines of the Eight Expression, very often overpowers the individual's spiritual vision and good sense, entrapping the person in a web and loop of dishonesty, deceit, illusion, fraud, usury, misrepresentation and general untoward behavior, a spiritually tragic scenario. The Great Law of Karma - the pure embodiment of cosmic law - brings back to everyone that which is generated and perpetrated. What we sow, we reap.

Poisonous seeds bear only poisonous fruit, while nourishing seeds bear life-giving nourishing fruit. Manipulation for personal gain, therefore, only spells trouble for the manipulator. He may be successful in the short run, but his negative karma will catch up to him eventually. It is interesting to note that the word "karma" is itself an Eight.

```
K  A  R  M  A
2  1  9  4  1  =  17  >  1 + 7  =  8
```

The Eight Expression would best be served to focus on making positive connections which yield positive results for itself and others. Eights need to be the 'mover'. Be the 'doer'. Be the 'connector'. Be the success-oriented person. Be the CEO, the executive, leader, manager, commander, principal, president, coordinator, but. . . do not misuse or violate the special integrative, interconnective, managerial social skills and talents inherent in the Eight energy. Walk a karmically tight line. What the Eight person does will return to him in spades. Therefore, the admonition is to play the connective game of life well, but play it honestly and ethically and never forget that, "What goes around, comes around."

The 9 Expression

As a Nine Expression, you manifest a power and charisma unlike any of the other eight basic vibrations. Nine is the final vibratory experience of the soul as it journeys through the numerical Avenue of Crowns - the singe digit numbers One through Nine, aka, the alpha-numeric spectrum. Since Nine is the

Grand Elemental, being a composite of the nine single digits, it contains all vibrations within it and, therefore, understands and identifies and is understood and identified by all (see *The King's Book of Numerology, Volume I: Foundations & Fundamentals*). Thus, Nine is the vibration of all people, the 'many', the masses, the public stage, the universal theater of man.

The Nine Expression spans many areas of life's universal theater and is, in fact, a prime vibration within the specific arena of the artistic theater, drama, radio, and television. But it is also present in the healing arts, literary arts, language arts, musical arts, metaphysical arts, martial arts and all creative and performing arts in general. Notice the word, 'Art'. Nine is definitely artistic and it is no accident that it spans all cultures, all races, all geographical, financial, social, ethnic, environmental and governmental boundaries.

The Nine Expression maintains an expanded focus, often national, international and global in dimension. As a Nine Expression, you are a person for all people because you understand all people and people consciously or subconsciously identify with you. You have a natural charisma that radiates even when you just stand still. Your vibratory essence rules. You are strong, dominant, powerful.

This natural power and strength of the Nine is one of its greatest assets. It is also one of its greatest liabilities. Although Nine dominates, it can also be domineering to its detriment. No one likes a bully or one who abuses his power, authority or position. As Lord Acton wrote in a letter to Bishop Mandell Creighton (5 April 1887), "Power tends to corrupt and absolute power corrupts absolutely." Charles Caleb Colton declares, "No man is wise enough, nor good enough to be trusted with unlimited power" (1825). Percy Shelley, the famous English poet of the Nineteenth Century, muses in Queen Mab, "Power, like a desolating pestilence, pollutes whatever it touches." This is one of the dangers of the Nine Expression: it can be corrupt, arrogant, imperious, overbearing and powerfully destructive. Therefore, Nine people need to keep a tight rein/reign on their actions.

To illustrate this principle of the abuse of power, there is a story in spiritual annals of a queen who ruled oppressively, her tyrannical nature causing much hardship, pain, suffering and anguish in the lives of her subjects, souls she was given to serve. As a result of spending her life in being a wicked and ignoble queen, in her next life God gave her the incarnation and form of a donkey, a beast of burden. Her punishment - to carry the burdens of others on her back for her entire life as she had caused others to be burdened by her when she was in the role of the ruler queen.

This is a poignant story. In the grand spiritual scope of creation, we never know what the divine purpose of our present incarnation is. Perhaps we are given the role of a ruler - a king, queen, president, prime minister, executive, magistrate, manager, law-enforcement officer, judge, etc., to determine, from a spiritual perspective, if we are capable of handling the power that comes when one is placed in such a position to ascertain our worth in receiving more and greater spiritual power. God is always testing our soundness. Worldly power may just be a test to see if we are capable of managing spiritual power. If we misuse the power associated with some little earthly position, how could we possibly be granted the responsibility of power associated with spiritual ascendance?

Regardless of the position or vibration in which our Expression is cast, we can never forget for one moment that we are accountable for everything we do, say or think and, in one way or another, at one time or another, we will pay for our abuses, our indiscretions, crimes, negative behaviors and untoward actions. Karmic Law is inviolable and infinitely more powerful than any of the Nine basic vibrations including the Nine. Thus, it is always important to take the high road but the low ground, especially if we, during this life, walk in the cloak and carry the scepter of the Nine Expression. Nine rules, but it may rule to its detriment and, if not careful, guarantee, by its abuse of power, future lives and incarnations of oppressive personal slavery in the form of a donkey perhaps, as our previous story illustrates, or even in other ways as Karmic Law dictates. Therefore Nines, be wise. Rule well. Your actions will become your executioner or liberator.

As the Six expression loves personally, the Nine Expression loves impersonally. Its focus is on the masses, not the solitary individual, save the fact that each person is a part of the great whole. Nine is not a domestic energy. It is a public, universal energy. It moves on the public stage of life, its true and natural home.

When its energy rises to its highest level, the Nine Expression is the humanitarian, the universal giver, the loyal, devoted, committed servant of the people and the common good. Nine is often seen, therefore, in the charts of teachers, religious leaders, doctors, nurses, dentists, social workers, philanthropists and all types of occupations in which contact with the public is standard operating procedure. Nine touches all people, serves all people, embraces all people because it is all people.

As a Nine Expression, enjoy your charisma. Enjoy your talents. Enjoy your power and strength. Enjoy the grand stage of life. Enjoy mixing and moving among the world's many and varied peoples. Love your artistic side. Embellish your humanitarian side. Be the gracious, grand, magnanimous, generous, universal giver. This is you at your best. Rule well and remember that true rulership is based on service, not dominance; on meeting the needs of others, not satisfying your own. Teach, entertain, help, heal, uplift, serve, rule. "Only the highest can help the lowest," says Saint Charan Singh. As a Nine Expression, you hold, at least temporarily in this incarnation, an exalted position. Exalt Him. Serve Him and others and you, too, will be exalted. But. . . abuse your power and position and you, too - yes, even you, will be abused in time through the very Law that placed you where you are. Karmic Law, the Ruler in this dimension of polar opposites.

Chapter Four

THE PERFORMANCE
[The Role in Life]

As the Lifepath represents the script of our lives and the Expression denotes us as the actor or actress, the Performance-Experience [PE] represents exactly that, the performance we will give on the life stage. In effect, this PE is the *role* we give in life. If one hundred actors were given the same script, when each performer acted out the script, the performance [or role] each actor would give would be different from all the rest because of the individual personalities, talents, traits, and attributes each actor/actress brings to the script. Like snowflakes, no two performances would be identical. In fact, it is safe to say that no two performances given by the same actor/actress would be exactly the same.

Hence, the Performance-Experience or PE is the role we give in life. It is not the script. It is not us. It is the *performance* we give as a result of us, the actor/actress (Expression), reading and playing out the life-script we were given at birth (Lifepath). The Performance-Experience is simply derived through addition of the Lifepath and Expression.

The Performance/Experience [PE] Formula

Lifepath [LP] + Expression [Exp] = Performance/Experience [PE]

When an

ACTOR
(Numerology label: *Expression*)
(Derived from the Natal Name)

Reads a
↓

SCRIPT
(Numerology label: *Lifepath*)
(Derived from the Birthdate data)

He gives a
↓

PERFORMANCE
(Numerology label: *P/E or Performance/Experience*)
(Derived from adding the Expression to Lifepath)

Since we've already created the Lifepath [LP] number [Chapter Two] and the Expression [Chapter Three], this Performance cipher is very quick to calculate. Simply add the two together and reduce to a single digit if necessary. For example, if your Lifepath is a 4 and your Expression is a 2, your Performance number is a 6.

4 Lifepath + 2 Expression = 6 PE

If your Lifepath is a 7 and your Expression is an 8, your PE is a 6.

7 Lifepath + 8 Expression = 15 > 1 + 5 = 6 PE.

How long did that take? Five seconds, maybe? Super simple.

Let's calculate the Performance number for our imaginary friends, Mary Jane Smith and John David Doey. Mary's Lifepath is a 7; her Expression is a 3. Therefore, her PE is a 1.

7 Lifepath + 3 Expression = 10 > 1 + 0 = 1.

Mary Jane Smith's Performance Experience [PE] is a 1.

John's Lifepath is a 9; his Expression is a 1. His PE is also a 1.

9 Lifepath + 1 Expression = 10 > 1 + 0 = 1

John David Doey's Performance Experience [PE] is a 1.

Now it's your turn. What's your Performance Experience [PE]?

Your Lifepath ____ + Your Expression ____ = _____ PE

In numerology, the ability of distinguishing the individual from the role being performed is critical to understanding the specific person. In most instances, the person and the role are two very different entities. The Expression is the person, the actor. The Performance-Experience or PE is the role that person is playing. The PE is, indeed, the performance that particular individual is giving during this life time, but, in most cases, the performance <u>is not</u> the person. It is simply the reality that person is experiencing at the present time by way of the script being acted out and performed by the person in question. The rub, of course, is that the PE seems so real because, in effect, the person is living the role, not simply acting it out in a superficial way as one would do on stage.

For example, let's assume one maintains a Six (6) Expression and an Eight (8) Lifepath. Through addition of these two components of the Basic Matrix, the Performance-Experience would be a Five (5) [$6 + 8 = 14 > 1 + 4 = 5$]. The Five PE would showcase this person in a role of freedom, movement, change and adventure, seemingly unconcerned and detached from issues regarding family, domesticity, personal love, home and community - all attributes of the Six. Yet, because the Expression represents the person specifically and not the role he or she is playing, the attributes of the Six - heart, hearth and home - are precisely what this person is all about, even though the Five PE offers a different and more contrasting picture.

Because our role in life, as represented by our Performance-Experience [Reality] cipher, is so very visible to others, we must be careful not to mis-assess ourselves or others. A person may have a One [1] Expression, making him very individualistic and assertive, yet be giving a performance of support and passivity as represented by a Two [2] PE. This would, of course, indicate a One [1] Lifepath [1 Expression + 1 Lifepath = 2 PE]. If we are not careful, we may incorrectly assess the person as being passive and submissive because of the 2 PE when, in effect, this is simply the role the person is playing and not a representation of who the person is as represented by the One Expression. In a larger sense, of course, all of it - the Expression and PE - is who we are, for even though the PE is a performance, it is, nonetheless, our performance and no other's. Still, be aware there is a difference between actor/actress and the role being performed on the great life stage.

Performance Descriptions

Note: The Performance-Experience [PE] descriptions are the same as those for the Expression. If you have a Nine [9] Lifepath, your Expression will read the same as your PE. Why? Because the number 9 when added to any number always equals that same number. We saw this in the example of John David Doey whose Lifepath is a 9 and Expression is a 1. For example, a person like John with a 1 Expression [Exp] and a 9 Lifepath [LP] will have a 1 PE.

$$9 \text{ Lifepath} + 1 \text{ Expression} = 10 > 1 + 0 = 1 \text{ PE}$$

Just keep in mind that the PE is the *role* in life and the Expression is the *person*. There is a difference. In fact, distinguishing a person's Expression from his PE can be a fun exercise, especially if their PE is drastically different from their Expression.

The 1 Performance [PE or Role in Life]

As a person reflecting a One Performance, you definitely are an individual, your own person. You like to do things your way. You like to lead, not follow. In the family you may be a dominant patriarch or matriarch. In business or commerce, you need to be out front as the boss, manager or employer. You may also be the pioneer, following the beat of your own drum, exploring areas, ideas and concepts unknown to the rest of the masses. You have ideas and can generate them, for you are ruled by the element fire which is always active, alive, vibrant, warming. You are unique, and there is great potential for you to be especially creative with your mind and with words. You are a doer, an activator and initiator, one who gets the ball rolling and the project underway. You do like to be out front, in the lead where all can follow you or be in the center where you are the focus of attention. You do not like to share the spotlight as a general rule. You may well be an entrepreneur in the commercial/business arena.

In the One Performance there is great emphasis on the self, your self. This is fine if you do not allow the dominant, powerful, creative, vibrant One energy to become too self-absorbed and individually all-consuming. The highest expression of the One is union with the Divine. The lowest expression is negative egomania where one feels the entire world and universe revolve around him or her - a totally self-centered, self-consumed, self-absorbed, arrogant, imperious, egomaniacal, overbearing, unbending dictator. To keep the One humble, it must be remembered that there is only one true One and that is God from whom all the other little ones originate, and He may, at His slightest whim, expunge any little one who is not reflecting the majesty, truth, grandeur, creativity and oneness of His One.

Therefore, as a One Performance, there is great responsibility on your shoulders. You can reflect the majesty of His Oneness through a process of merging with Him, or you can reflect the distasteful arrogance of the little one trying to be a big-shot. The latter would be a result of separation, not union, with the Divine. But One is Union, not separation, so the only feasible solution is to deny the little ego by acknowledging the only Ego - His Ego, His Presence. A One Performance may live life, therefore, as the drop of water separate from the ocean or as the drop which has merged with the ocean, thereby, reflecting its power and beauty.

On a more human note, Ones have strong wills. This is important from a leadership position. As a leader, One must take a stand and lead, not bend and break or worse, descend into the flock where confusion and chaos will possibly reign if there is no leadership, if there is no one with the strength, conviction, wherewithal and basic guts to stand up and say, "Follow me!" Leadership is always a lonely, frightening, uncomfortable, solitary experience because the leader is out front for all to see, acclaim or defame. However, it's easy to criticize from the pack, especially if the burden of leadership is on someone else's shoulders. Being a leader means making tough decisions and having the courage to stick by them. Leadership is additionally difficult because it is impossible to please all the people all the time. It's a rough and tough job but society must have leaders and this is one of the potential roles for the person who reflects the One Performance.

As a leader, the fundamental precept to follow is simply to act on the principle of Oneness. We are all part of a whole, one united Being with multiple hands and feet. A man may be an island, but nobody is a world. We all exist together on one planet, one shrinking planet, where, eventually, everyone must learn to act as one, not two, if for no other reason than basic global survival. We are, indeed, one world. The true leader is the one who sees this and creates oneness, not separateness; who creates union, not disunion.

The strength of will of the One Performance becomes negative when the one becomes so rigid it does not bend. However, One must bend at times, just not break. Take, for example, the solitary and beautiful willow tree. It stands strong and alone but its branches bend to accommodate the wind. In other words, it gives in where it has to. This does not diminish it, for the tree sustains no damage from the wind. Its inherent structure simply allows it to bend and survive.

Another aspect of the One Performance is the self. Self is an important concept but, once again, the self has two sides: one positive; one negative. The positive self is the one 'at one' with its Source. The negative one is the one separate from its Source and acting independently. This may seem enigmatic but it is not. In the realm of separate entities, as all of us are in the worldly scheme of things, we naturally possess a unique individuality. But we are nothing without a common Source uniting us all. To illustrate this, we can simply see each of us as a separate light bulb - unique, separate, individual - but, nonetheless, a bulb like every other bulb which receives its brilliance from one source - the electric current. Without the current, each bulb, each of us, is lightless and lifeless. Yes, we are individuals but we all run on the same current and derive our life energy from the same Source.

Another example is that we are all bubbles floating on the surface of the ocean. Yes, we are separate but not dis-separate from our Source once again. Furthermore, as a bubble, our life span is not very long. Thus, why get too involved with our fleeting individuality? It is temporal at best. When we die and if we are reincarnated in a human form, we will get another name and identity - another ego. So why become overly involved with this one or any one for that matter? It is best, therefore, to identify with the one Current which gives us life, to identify with the vast Ocean of the Spirit from which we gain our true identity, our true self.

The One Performance is a masculine energy. Does this mean that a female maintaining a One Performance is not feminine? No. Quite the contrary. It simply means that she will tend to be more logical and reasonable than she might otherwise be, as logic and reason are male/yang characteristics. She will, as a One Performance, naturally possess energies of leadership, creation, initiation and action. She will be self-motivated, will take charge and get things done without being told to if she is in a support role as a secretary, assistant or helper of some kind. If she is in a prime leadership role as a manager, president or executive, she has the inherent ability to lead exceptionally well by infusing her One Performance male/yang energy with her inherent Two female/yin energy. Male One Performance leaders run the risk of being too overbearing and dominant because of the concentration of one energy. A female, on the other hand, can balance the male yang energy of leadership with her intrinsic female yin energy of support, caring, nurturing and compassion. She must simply avoid being too vacillating, which is a female/yin characteristic. Leaders of any sex may change their minds, but they cannot be vacillatory nor illogical or overly emotional if they choose to be effective. Leadership requires action and courage and the best of all leadership is that which is balanced by both male and female energies.

As a One Performance, enjoy your uniqueness, for you are unique and original. Enjoy your independence. Enjoy your creative abilities. Be excited by your ability to take action and to lead. Not everyone can act, create, generate, initiate and lead as you do. But do not look down on others because they are not leaders or because they cannot create or take action. That's your job, at least in this life. A leader needs followers; followers need leaders. Neither is more important than the other. It's all part of the whole polarity scene of this creation. Be wary of becoming too self-centered. It is best to be divinely Self-Centered, i.e., acknowledging God as the only True One which He obviously is.

The 2 Performance [PE or Role in Life]

As a person reflecting a Two Performance, you are one who supports, helps, cares for and sustains others. You have compassion, kindness and a gentleness of manner. Your passive nature allows you to be unobtrusive, soft, friendly, congenial, agreeable, cordial, conciliatory, cooperative and comprising. Because you are ruled by the Two, you can generally see both sides of an issue and often serve as a peacemaker or diplomat. Your emotional energy brings feelings to situations where pure logic and reason are found lacking. You tend to be intuitive and receptive, flowing and working with situations rather than attempting to impose your will and ego on others. You are considered the peacemaker of the alpha-numeric spectrum.

The Two Performance is governed by the female yin energy of the universe. You are a follower by nature, giving those dominated by One energy a chance to lead and experience the lesson of the self. You tend to be subordinate and possibly submissive but this does not make you less important in the least. After all, cosmic, universal structure is comprised of two distinct energies - the One and the Two, the yang and the yin. Neither is more important than the other. They both comprise the whole. But they do have different qualities and characteristics which are, in fact, opposite and oftentimes contrapuntal, if not contentious by their very nature.

The Two Performance is centered in relationships. This is why women, and men with a Two Performance or other Two energy in their charts, are more in tune with relationships than men in general or women dominated by a strong One influence. Females are ruled by this number Two energy of relationships whereas males, who are ruled by the number One, live in the world of ideas and action. Women live in the world of others and reaction. One is day. Two is night. Both are ends of the same continuum. Both are critical to the cosmic structure. However, neither men or women are purely yang (male) or yin (female). Both sexes are a blend of One and Two energy, although One energy is generally associated with men and Two energy with women.

The Two energy is powerful in its ability to support. This is why women have often been characterized as the "power behind the throne," especially in the past. But all that is changing. Women are now moving to the forefront of society where they will be the "power on the throne."

An interesting cosmic note is that our earth has entered the Second Millennium from a numerological perspective. This means that the Two energy will be highlighted. Thus, a person with a Two Performance will feel more comfortable in this millennium than in the First Millennium where the number One dominated. The cosmic pendulum has now swung the other way. We have experienced a thousand years of the One male energy of the yang and it is now time for the earth to experience the Two female energy of the yin - a very opposite polarity with opposite attributes and characteristics.

This polar shift is one of the main reasons we see such confusion in our world today. All of us alive at this time, particularly those born before the year 2000, or who have parents or friends who were, are experiencing, either directly or indirectly, both of these contrasting polar vibrations of the One and Two! As explained in *The Age of the Female: A Thousand Years of Yin* [available at www.richardking.net], those souls born after the year 2031 will only know the polar vibration of the Two. Hence, they will not know by direct experience the vibration of the One except vicariously through the eyes and tongues of those of us who were born in the nineteen hundreds. Thus, they will not have the understanding of having lived in both yang and yin vibratory periods. That gift, if it can be called that, is reserved only for those who have lived in the Twentieth and Twenty-First centuries, quite a distinction when one thinks about it. What other souls in creation can claim this unique experience?

The Two Performance will obviously harmonize with the Second Millennium. As the Two Performance is focused in the realm of 'others', so the Second Millennium will be one of 'others' as well. This will not be a time glorifying the sovereignty of isolated and separate nations and people. This will be a time of learning to get along with others, to share our world, to be concerned about what others do in the scheme of world balance, health and equilibrium. Relationships will be important, relationships that engender peace and harmony.

One of the cautions of the Two Performance rests in its quality of duality. At its spiritual zenith, Two rules balance, peace, compassion, equilibrium and harmony. However, at its negative nadir, it is a vibration of opposition, competition, contention, conflict, imbalance, hostility, antagonism, disunity, separation, argumentation and friction. The number Two can be viewed as the analogy of the tug-o-war with both sides, both polar extremes, pulling equally from both directions. The Two can also be viewed as the teeter-totter in constant imbalance, rising and falling in almost perpetual motion. This is why the Two is viewed as emotional - it lacks one continuous motion: i.e., "e-motion" - out of motion, out of His One Perfect Motion, Speed and Rhythm.

Thus, as a Two Performance, you must guard against this polarization creating imbalance, inharmony and contention. You have the ability to generate great peace, harmony, kindness and compassion, but like all vibrations, the Two also has its opposite side, and the opposite of harmony is inharmony; the opposite of balance is imbalance; the opposite of peace is war.

One unites. Two separates and divides. In our society today, we probably have more separate and distinct factions than at any other time in world history. And the number seems to be growing. Under the Two vibration, people divide into groups and take sides. These sides oppose each other and will oppose each other until everyone learns that harmonious life is the result of balance, the positive aspect of the Two, not destructive opposition, its negative aspect.

The beauty of the Two lies in expressing unity, not disunity. This is the challenge of the Second Millennium. It is also the challenge of the Two Performance. Make peace, not war. Create harmony, not disharmony. Think of others, not of self. Respect those who support and serve, not just those who lead while being maintained by the support of others. Cooperate; don't dominate. Compromise. Find the Golden Mean, the middle ground between polarities. Create peace. This is the great calling for the Two Performance.

For more information on the number Two and its dominance of the current thousand years, read *The Age of the Female: A Thousand Years of Yin* and *The Age of the Female II: Heroines of the Shift* available at richardking.net.

The 3 Performance [PE or Role in Life]

As a Three Expression you are definitely expressive. You are pleasant to be around. You smile a great deal of the time. You are friendly, easy to know, and emit a positive attitude. Generally, you like to talk, visit with friends, socialize. Words may be an important part of who you are. You may like to write, especially if you also maintain some dominant Seven energy in your chart. You are most probably very attractive and there is an excellent chance you will be associated with the arts in some capacity - this to fulfill your personal sense of self-expression and communication. If your personal Expression is elevated to the nineties decade with a 93 root, you may well want to express yourself on the public stage of life or, perhaps, even in the theater as an actor or actress. If your General Expression is rooted in the eighties decade with an 84 root, your Three Expression will most likely be manifested in the world of business and commerce. If your Three has a sixty-six root, you may well love to sing or use your voice to bring love and harmony to others. You may also be driven to write, to express your thoughts and deepest feelings on paper as a journalist, playwright, sports writer, composer, fiction or non-fiction author. Your mental skill with words could also propel you into the television milieu as a commentator, news-anchor, reporter, host or announcer. As a Three Expression, communication in some capacity is vital to your being. For more information regarding the Expression and its root structures, read *The King's Book of Numerology, Volume I: Foundations & Fundamentals*).

The key word to describe you though is self-expression. Even if you do not use words as much as other Threes, you may find yourself visually expressing and communicating your talent in the health and beauty field, perhaps as a model, beautician, make-up artist, clothes designer, etc. How you integrate your body, mind and spirit is important to you, for the Three is the cosmic vibration which completes the male-female, positive-negative polar connection. This is reflected in the symbol of the triangle which is the ancient symbol for perfection. In the triangle we can see the balance of the One and Two energy being brought together to create a completed circuit. When this cosmic circuit is completed, balance between the opposing polarities is created and one becomes happy, fulfilled and expressive as a natural extension of a balanced condition. Where there is balance, there is peace and ease, no contention, friction or stress generated as a result of opposing polarities pulling and tugging on each other.

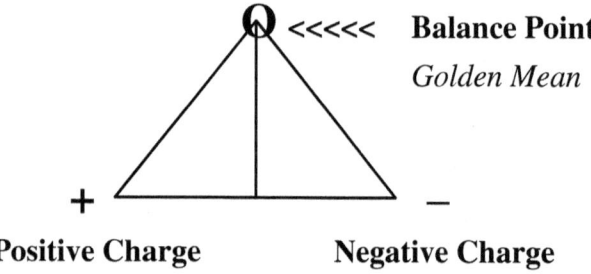

This balanced state is the reason the Three vibration is seen as that basic vibration generating the most ease of the nine major energy fields. As a Three Performance, you are a person who generates this ease, comfort, like-ability, friendliness and fun.

The number Three is also the number of the Trinity: Father, Son and Holy Ghost; Master, Disciple and Word. Therefore, an individual with a divinely elevated sense of this cosmic vibration may well be involved spiritually or religiously, expressing the divine connection and integration which is intrinsic to the Three vibration. In fact, this aspect of the Three is the reflection of its greatest meaning - divine integration of the body, mind and spirit which moves and ascends upward toward the Divine apex.

Since all vibrations have their negative side, as certainly as the Three can bring integration, ease, health and beauty, it can also bring disintegration, dis-ease, sickness and ugliness of one sort or another. Negative self-expression, self-harm, self-mutilation or self-destruction are possible with a negatively aspected Three, as well as being unlikable in a social sense. What can be perfect can also be imperfect. Beauty, like sickness, does not last forever. Happiness, in a worldly context, is as ephemeral as sadness. Remember, the cosmic pendulum swings both ways, and where there is health, there is also the potential of disease.

In consideration of this cosmic fact, when we have or reflect enjoyment, ease, comfort, beauty and friends, we must not forget the spiritual purpose of life - that of God-Realization. Too often when situations, conditions and times, or our personal self-expression, are good, pleasant, enjoyable and fulfilling, we forget our Divine Roots, much to our eventual chagrin. We can be thrown off the mark, off the balance beam, just as easily by joy as by tragedy. Balance, represented by the Golden Mean, the middle ground of the triangle, should not be forgotten. Rather, it should be the focus of the Three energy, for ultimately the Three Performance is about personal expression through Divine Integration, not wanton and self-indulgent pleasure.

There are three cautions with the Three Performance. The first is excessive vanity. The number Three rules image, and if one's personal image is not controlled it will expand to destructive degrees. It is important to have a healthy self-image, no doubt, but when carried to extremes that image becomes very distasteful.

A second caution is entitlement. Three rules ease of living, comfort, joy and good fortune. Such things are wonderful blessings, but they should not be taken for granted or expected. Sometimes having too much of a good thing can be a curse as much as a blessing. Such good fortune should not be flaunted or imposed upon others with thoughtless disregard and egocentric abandon. We do reap what we sow, and sowing entitlement and ingratitude will result in good fortune being taken away.

A third caution is over-indulgence in pleasure. Three rules pleasure of all kinds, but when that pleasure is focused too much in the material world, the results will be painfully tragic. Over-indulgence in alcohol, drugs, sex and personal power is the harbinger of a great fall. Numerology archives are filled with cases of individuals whose lives were destroyed because of unchecked wanton self-indulgence. Societies have collapsed because of the same situation. Certainly, Rome had its issues with over-indulgence in its higher echelons of society which contributed to its downfall. For an individual desirous of a contented life, it must be remembered that the flip side of pleasure is pain, and the more pleasure is sought for, the more pain will be experienced. As Saint Charan Singh has stated:

> *No matter how great the pleasures of the world may be, they are not only short lived but they have equally unpleasant reactions at some time or another.*

Therefore, as has been mentioned repeatedly, balance is primary in all things.

As a positively charged Three Performance, it's important to share your sense of joy and happiness with others. A smile, a laugh, a good word, a sincere ear and a few light-hearted moments go a long way in easing other people's worries. Your joy is infectious. Let it shine.

Too, be the artist you intrinsically are. Write, sing, paint, debate, sculpt, act, compose, model. Let the joyous strings, pipes, drums and ivory keys of your basic nature fill other people with your positive energy. You are an artist after all, a communicator, a bringer of joy, hope and happiness. We all need you, especially in a world where joy and happiness are such rare commodities.

The 4 Performance [PE or Role in Life]

The Four Performance is the rock and salt of the earth. Four is the vibration representing the structures of our lives - physically, mentally, emotionally, socially, maritally, financially. If your Four Performance is not negatively aspected in your chart, you are a solid, dependable, reliable, hard-working, trustworthy, devoted, service-oriented individual who is more rooted than any of the other nine vibrations. You are an anchor, and people depend on you often to anchor them and give them strength. The ultimate expression of the Four energy is one of service, work and effort, moving, sometimes plodding, along with undiminished regularity and dogged persistence.

Your Four Performance may be expressed in the creative field as a painter, sculptor, designer, photographer. The Four energy constructs, especially in the world of form, so your artistic abilities may take shape as great works of tangible or visual art.

The symbol of the Four is the square and represents the foundations and structures of our lives. Depending upon our perspective, we can stand on top of the square, using it as a foundation; be protected and guarded by it by dwelling within the security of its walls, or be crushed by its weight by existing below it. Therefore, how we use our Four energy is vital to our sense of strength and security. All of these locations in relation to the square can give security. However, they can also give a sense of limitation and imprisonment because the Four, unlike the Five, does not move or change. It stays put, rooted in place like the Rock of Gibraltar.

The Three Placements of the Square

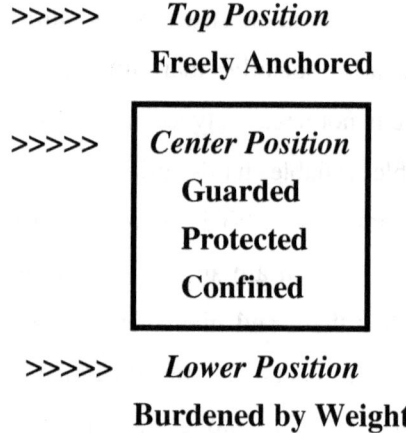

>>>>>   *Top Position*
        Freely Anchored

>>>>>   *Center Position*
        Guarded
        Protected
        Confined

>>>>>   *Lower Position*
        Burdened by Weight

In the Top Position, we are anchored to life but free enough to experience the world around us. In the Center Position, we are confined within the square. Depending upon our make-up, this may be comforting or confining. In the Lower Position, we are burdened by the weight of the Four, perhaps even feeling crushed by the mass of its vibrations. We may even experience all three positions at once or at separate times. The point is that we will feel the weight and gravity of the Four, positively or negatively.

Positive Fours are very secure people; rock solid and oozing with control, dependability, reliability and trust. Negative Fours often violate the principle of structure in their lives and become imprisoned or pressed down by its weight. For example, if a person is not trustworthy, is not reliable, is not dependable, is not faithful, is not disciplined, is not controlled, then only trouble can ensue.

The great vibration of the Four Performance demands structure, control and the purity, persistence, effort and sacrifice of action and behavior characteristic of the long-suffering of Noah and his family during the forty days of rain upon the earth and the forty days of the Flood; of Moses and his people in the desert for forty years, of Moses himself on Mount Sinai for forty days and nights and, of course, Jesus in the wilderness for forty days. Forty, whose crown is the Four, is the vibration representing purification through discipline, determination, self-control, restraint, continence, work, effort, toil, limitation, regimentation, regulation, order, sacrifice and unrelenting persistence. When these qualities are learned and expressed, the result is ultimate strength and security. But make no mistake, there can be no strength and security without the aforementioned virtues. Strength is, itself, a virtue but it can not be manifested without those qualities which comprise its structure and which give it form.

One of the hazards of the Four Performance is being so overly consumed with the principle of 'structure' that one becomes stuck in the mud, unable to move and change when one's best interest may call for some type of adaptation to the structure, maybe even to leave the structure like a snake shedding its skin. Some Fours can be so stubborn and resistant at times they give new meaning to the word 'jack ass'. If, for example, one believes in loyalty, he is under no law to jump off a cliff at the behest of another person, taking his life in the process, however strongly he believes in loyalty. God does not condone suicide under any circumstances. A person, however, who is overly saturated with a misguided sense of devotion and loyalty, may not have the good, common and divine sense to see outside the box and make the proper adjustments and take the proper actions to protect his ultimate divine security. It is good to be rooted but not so immovable that one jeopardizes his health and well-being in the process or that of others. Thus, the balanced Four Performance needs to reflect practicality but not be impractical.

You are a Four Performance. Be strong. Be secure. Be stable. Be practical. Be disciplined. Be dependable, reliable, trustworthy, loyal, faithful, devoted. Work hard - there can be no excellence without effort. Live by a code of life, a living structure of rules and regulations. Serve life because you are the great servant. Keep your priorities in line and forever. . . be the rock!

The 5 Performance [PE or Role in Life]

As a Five Performance, you are the epitome of motion, movement, change, experience, adventure and versatility. You love your freedom and do not like to be restricted. Unlike the Four Expression which plants roots and seeks a grounded stability, you generally have few roots and prefer stability in motion. Your love of freedom makes you seem unstable at times but stability is a relative concept. An airplane in flight, for example, is not stable in a 'grounded' sense but quite stable in a moving/flying sense. In fact, it needs the movement of the air over its wings to keep it stable. Motion and movement are critical to its balance, health and well-being. Without such motion, the plane would crash and burn. As a Five Performance, you are much like an airplane - motion not only makes you free, but it keeps you stable. Therefore, do not worry about those who see you as unstable. You simply have a different functional understanding of stability.

Change is important to you. The movement you need in your life is not simply physical movement, it is psychological, social, vocational, sexual, emotional, and spiritual as well. You thrive on new experiences because they feed your desire to know more, explore more, do more. Change, constant change, is the vehicle through which you acquire this experience. This also makes you talented in many areas. Doing one thing is not enough for you. You need the input of varied stimuli to keep you alive and excited. If you receive this stimulation, your Five energy is complete and you feel satisfied. If there is too little stimulation, you wither and wane. You are not meant to be the rock, confined to one place your whole life. You are meant to be the eagle, to fly, to soar, to be free, to ride the ever-changing winds of life, enthralled with the majesty of motion in flight.

As a Five Performance, you may definitely have many talents and be a person for all people (see *The King's Book of Numerology, Volume I: Foundations & Fundamentals*). You will be a person who loves to socialize with friends, seeking pleasure and good times. You will possibly enjoy exploring things mentally, psychologically and spiritually if you also have Seven energy supporting your Five. There is the distinct possibility your sense of movement in the arena of the heart, romance, the home and family will give you many experiences, adventures and lessons in freedom and detachment.

As a Five Performance, you must guard against over indulgence in sensual pleasures of all kinds. The Five loves to experience and explore but some things are better left unexplored and inexperienced. Who, in their right mind, would ever want to be sucked into the dark abyss of a black hole? Yet, there are many black holes in this world. Not all experiences are positive, let alone spiritual, and many experiences lead to incarceration, not freedom. Alcohol, drugs and illicit sexuality are black holes to the soul. Free indulgence in them leads to imprisonment in the world of the senses from which escape is extremely difficult. In effect, nothing is free. Everything has a price. Never forget that. In spite of contemporary thought and wishful thinking, there is no such thing as free love, free drinks, free anything. We simply must pay for everything we get in life. Neglecting spiritual law and its edict of discipline, self-control and temperance leads to imprisonment, and imprisonment is not a pleasant, comfortable or enjoyable experience. If the Five is not careful, it will rue the day it sought too much experience after demanding too much freedom and over-indulging its sensual appetite when it should have exercised more discipline and restraint. As Pythagoras said, *No man is free who cannot control himself.* More than any other number, the Five needs to heed this lesson.

Therefore, for the Five Performance, discretion and a positive sense of discrimination - the ability to discern what is healthful or harmful, is critical for this freedom-loving, experiencing-seeking explorer and adventurer. Learning to make right choices to advance one's spiritual evolution is more important than simply making a choice to be free and experiential. If we can <u>pro</u>gress in our life's journey, we can also <u>re</u>gress. Where we go and where we will be tomorrow depends upon the choices we make today, now, in the present, for as certain as the sun shines, there will be consequences to our every action and we will have to pay the price for the things and experiences we choose to buy.

The Five vibration must be seen and understood correctly from a spiritual perspective. The Five loves freedom but true freedom is based on and is the product of extreme discipline, regulation, restriction and self-control. Unrestrained, unregulated, undisciplined action does not create freedom because all actions have their consequences, and the consequence of unrestrained behavior is captivity and destruction. Freedom is not "license carte blanche." Freedom is action taken in consideration of consequence.

As a Five Performance, you must carry this truth with you throughout your life, for the choices you make today will determine where you are tomorrow. The Five offers great freedom of choice but its inherent danger is that those choices could send you just as easily to heaven as to hell. Freedom is wonderful, but the abuse of freedom will send the soul into the darkest and most horror-filled dungeons imaginable. Therefore, use discretion, discrimination and foresight in making every choice at every step along the path of your life. Look ahead at the possible consequences to your actions *before* you take them. And remember, those choices promising fulfillment and satiation of and by the senses, although pleasurable and easy to make, often take the soul down a nether road to a dark and sorrow-filled land where freedom, even as a word, doesn't exist.

Fives must be careful also of becoming too scattered and too free, just as the Four must be careful of becoming too stable, too rooted. Balance is the key in all things. Because the Five moves at breakneck speed, it must be careful it doesn't fall and break its own neck. It is not uncommon for Fives to be accident-prone because they are doing so much so quickly they forget to concentrate on the task at hand. It's fine to move fast but one cannot afford to lose his concentration, just as a race car driver cannot afford to lose his. And Fives do like speed. Fast cars, fast horses, fast boats, fast planes, fast feet, fast intentions and fast experiences are part of the Five energy.

As a Five Performance, you are very personable. You like talking and visiting with others and can be extremely animated, charismatic, charming and dashing. Therefore, you would do well in fields involving the public and/or where you could move freely with little restriction. A nine-to-five job sitting in some back room or cubicle is not for you. Leave that to the Fours. You need a job in which you can be free to move about experiencing and sharing your talents with others. This does not mean you are irresponsible. Irresponsibility has nothing to do with freedom. It has to do with personal integrity. You can be as responsible as any other person. Nor does it mean you should lead a wanton, sensually-driven, libidinously saturated life in violation of spiritual law. You just cannot be constricted or restricted if you are to do your best work and be at your optimum health.

As a Five Performance, be free. Move. Fly. Change. It's okay to change. Experience. Enjoy your enthusiasm and let others enjoy it as well. But know the difference between true freedom and freedom carte blanche. Bad choices made under the superficial pretense of freedom can be painfully binding and bonding, relegating you, not to fields of freedom but to dungeons of bondage. True freedom, after all, detaches us from the world of form and phenomena, liberating us from this dimension of delusion and lifting us to higher skies where our spirit is unequivocally free of all dross and gross material trappings.

The 6 Performance [PE or Role in Life]

As a Six Performance, your entire being revolves around and is centered in your heart. Love of family, romance and close friends is extremely important to you. On a social level, you may well have a concern for the community as well. There is a softness about you, a gentleness which makes you the nurturer, the one who gives to others, embraces and supports them, keeping them warm and secure. If you are a female, you are the Mother of the Earth. If you are a male, you are the caring, compassionate patriarch. You enjoy beauty and harmony. Always, your heart remains at home.

As a Six Performance, you most likely are a lover of beauty. Six is a higher octave of two (the vibration of balance) and of three (the energy of beauty and integrated perfection). Six, therefore, is an amalgamation of these energies, expressing beauty, balance, creativity, harmony and sweetness.

As a Six, you most probably enjoy music very much and may even be an exquisite and exceptionally expressive performer. You may love to sing, creating beauty and harmony with your voice and words, soothing the tensions of others as well as yourself. Many great singers and performers have Six dominant in their numerology charts.

There is no doubt the home and domestic environment are intrinsically important to you. Devotion and loyalty are key. Six rules the home, heart and hearth and no other vibration is as attached or focused upon the domestic scene as you are. Trust your sense of being the loving parent and know that eight/ninths of the world does not have what you possess - a love of home and everything and everyone in it.

One of the attributes associated with the Six vibration is adjustment. Personal lives change, and as the lives of our loved ones change, as they will, the Six must adjust to keep everything in the home and heart balanced.

One red flag for the Six Performance is that while Six is the vibration of pure, personal, nurturing love, the opposite side of the coin is hate and its affiliate attributes of jealousy, envy, bitterness.

Love and hate are the positive and negative warp and woof of the tapestry of the Six vibration. In this dimension where one occurs, the other must also be present. This is why people in love often hurt, even kill, their lovers. Certainly, to walk the line of worldly love is to walk the razor's edge. Passion is passion and, although it can bring pleasure, it can also be manifested as displeasure in varying degrees. As a positive aside, just remember that people who hate you actually love you because their minds are always filled with you. They are absorbed with you, even though their thoughts and feelings may not be pleasant to us. When we hold a coin, we hold both sides simultaneously, so when the coin of love is in our hands, its flip side, hate, is also in our grasp. Another thing to remember is that the energy of hate is more destructive to the hater, the person who creates and holds the hate, than to anyone else. Hate is an extremely negative energy and is the cause of not only excessive dis-ease, but a myriad of diseases. As Saint Dariya of Bihar states: *The sower of the poison cannot but be engulfed in the poison.* And as Saint Ravidas confirms: *The fruit of action unfailingly overtakes the doer.* Excellent food for thought.

Six rules love. One expression of worldly love is lust, i.e. sexual gratification. Since Six is two times three and Three is the energy of pleasure, another red flag emerges. If one's romantic passions are not held in check, trouble can and often does arise with the Six Performance. It can even be far greater than that caused by the Three's misuse. Loving relationships, not lusting relationships, demand responsibility to both parties. However, one's passion for sexual gratification may often override one's loyalty to his or her significant other, the family and the community, bringing a wave of negative feedback, pain, sorrow, destruction and tears in the process. This is where the responsibility and devotion factors of the Six must come into play. Where there is responsibility, there is balance and beauty. Where there is irresponsibility, there is imbalance and ugliness.

It is, therefore, important to separate love from lust, love from passion. While many people say they are in love, they are really only expressing their passion, their carnal desires, their lust. Love, true love, elevates the soul. Passion (lust) debases the soul. Love purifies. Lust adulterates. Love always upgrades while lust degrades. Love cares about the highest and best good of those upon whom it is focused. Lust only cares for itself. Love would never jeopardize the health and well-being of another. Lust could care less for another's welfare.

Why is this important? Because Six Performance individuals have the ability to bring true personal love into manifestation. They can be the great mothers, the great fathers, the great nurturers of mankind; the true, devoted and loyal lovers who embrace the love of all in their hearts. Or. . . they can be the depraved and wanton libertines who use others to satisfy their own carnal and depraved appetites. As the Five Expression walks the road between freedom and slavery, the Six Performance walks the road between love and hate. We all have choices at every step, and those choices will determine our future. Such choices will also determine the love or hate we will receive in future lifetimes, as the Great Law of Karma is always operating in this dimension, returning to the doer the actions of his/hers deeds.

The 7 Performance [PE or Role in Life]

Seven Performance people are the most misunderstood of the nine basic expressions. They often seem aloof, cold, unconcerned, distant, untouchable. Yet, although they may be aloof from the wishes and whims of an externally-based society, they are extremely deep and in touch with the depths of their psyches. "Still waters run deep", and Sevens are deep. They are the thinkers of society, the ones who ponder, reflect, analyze, scrutinize. They do not care to be connected to the outer world because their connections are with the inner world. They know things others do not know or cannot know for they are deeply connected to the Force within.

This depth is manifested in their spiritual, religious, metaphysical behavior. It isn't that there is anything wrong with the outside world, it's just not their world. Their world is much more private, reclusive and isolated. Their need is to be alone and separate from others; to think, meditate, ponder, cogitate and reflect. Because most of the world is socially oriented, it does not understand Sevens and their need to be alone. But Sevens do understand themselves and that is all that is necessary. This separation from others appears to them that Sevens are cold, aloof and distant but Seven individuals are not cold, distant or aloof from the fiery spirit permeating their every pore. There is a reality within Seven individuals that those who live on the outside simply cannot understand nor appreciate. Therefore, Sevens create their own private space to pursue their interests and find their own peace.

These deep connections do not come without a price. That price is often the censure, criticism, ridicule and ostracism of others. Therefore, Sevens must be calm and serene to balance this unknowing of others and their possible untoward behavior toward them. They can't help themselves. They are just not deeply connected enough to understand how deep Seven people really are, how unconcerned they are with the external world and its superficial existence.

Thus, the Seven Performance person often finds himself alone. This state of isolation, and perhaps alienation, can be painful because even though he is deeply connected, he is still human and although he does not require the same external contact that others crave, it is difficult to be an isolated island within the stream of humanity. We all need contact with others and we have an intrinsic need to touch and be touched - not necessarily physically but emotionally and mentally. And here is where the Seven's special vibratory pattern shines. Because of its inward-dwelling sense of life, it has the ability to make the internal connection which those living in the external world cannot make. So the admonition of Seven people is, "do it." Make the internal, eternal connection. When this connection is made, there will be no more isolation because there will only be oneness, Oneness with God, the Creator of All that ever was, that is or will ever be. There is no connection greater than this and there is no connection giving such peace and everlasting bliss. Those who desire this divine peace must also travel the way of the Seven, for Seven is the key to the inner regions, to the Royal Realm where God resides.

Seven loves to have its space, and no number needs its own space more than the Seven. Others in its world need to know this so they can make the proper adjustments and keep the relationship harmonious. It is not that the Seven is not connected to others, it's just not connected to others in an external sense. Its depth of knowing can be a great anchor in other people's ocean of turmoil.

Seven is the vibration of supreme peace. Its opposite polarity is the vibration of supreme chaos. The Seven may be exhibiting one or the other polarity but the end to which it must aspire for its spiritual ascendancy is, of course, peace. This means it is necessary to stay centered in the eye of the hurricane where all is still and calm.

Pythagoras, the father of numerology, said Seven is the most sacred of all numbers because it's a synthesis of the trine of the spirit [ruled by the number Three] and the square of matter [ruled by the number Four]. Other world religions corroborate this fact of the Seven's sanctity, which is the most mentioned number in the Bible, especially in the Book of Revelation. In fact, the 3-4-7 triad is the most mentioned set of numbers in the Bible. Thus, a Seven Performance person is saturated with the potential of spirituality.

Carrying this further, it is worthy of note that one of the two numbers most often prevalent in the charts of substantively famous people whose reputations have stood the test of time is the number Seven. This is because Seven rules the spirit and it is the Spirit that every living soul has in common by divine decree. The Seven energy sensitizes us and makes us feel deeply, connecting with others in a way that is impossible for any other number. The other number prevalent in the charts of famous people is the Nine, the energy of universality, without whose energies it is difficult to obtain recognition and notoriety on the public stage.

Seven is not only the most potentially spiritual of all the numbers, it is also the most secretive and private. Sevens will always seek some degree of privacy. If they can't get it, they will create it by possibly starting a confrontation which they can use as a reason for some temporary separation. It's critical that people associated with a Seven person understand that the Seven person needs time alone because it's in their isolation that the Seven recharges and re-centers itself.

As far as secrecy goes, the Seven individual should be judicious and discerning. Some things are best left private, but secrecy can also create suspicion and have a negative effect on relationships. The foundation of all relationships is trust, and if the trust between people is destroyed because of secretive and untoward behaviors, the relationship may well be destroyed too.

Seven people can be very anal, i.e., overly meticulous. This is good for jobs requiring exactness and perfection. The problem arises when other people are not as meticulous and perceive the Seven person as being critical. Therefore, Sevens need to be cautious when dispensing help to others, and if they have to offer positive criticism to do so with warmth and tenderness.

The Seven is a very special number. It is intrinsically different from the other numbers in the alpha-numeric spectrum. Its goal is to be patient, appreciate its love of isolation and separation, seek perfection softly and go within where it is most at home and at peace.

The 8 Performance [PE or Role in Life]

As a positive Eight Performance, you are a person who loves to connect, interact and integrate. You are success-oriented, generally social by design, love money, wealth, status, power, position and social prominence. You can lead and manage well. You are not reclusive and introspective like the Seven, but outwardly driven, seeking to make yourself a worldly success. You can also work hard and efficiently, seeing what needs to be done and doing it. You are not just a worker. You are the one who orchestrates and coordinates the work, making things run smoothly - like a well-oiled machine. If you are an athlete, you are, no doubt, very coordinated and most likely the tops in your sport. As a performer, you know how to connect with your audience and with your subject matter. You are quite skilled at interacting with others which gives you a powerful social presence. You mix well with just about everyone. Success is vital to your well-being.

In many cases the Eight Performance will function smoothly in the world of business and commerce, focusing its energies in the fields of management, marketing, sales, advertising and finance.

The Eight Performance wants to integrate, connect and interact. As the highest octave of the 2-4-6-8 quartet, it is socially focused and likes to be involved in the external, worldly, social loop of success, wealth, riches, fame, name and power.

This interconnective attribute is expressed in the ancient lemniscate, the symbolic figure Eight representative of connection and 'flow' between the polar extremes of positive and negative charges. The lemniscate represents the cosmic energy loop connecting opposite polarities: male/female; buyer/seller, idea/manifestation, product/market, etc. A smooth flow is well-coordinated and efficient. When polar charges are brought together, there is success, a normal attribute of the Eight energy. It is the Eight Performance which reflects the function of this ancient symbol more than any other number. Eights love to be on the move, flowing in the loop of success, making the connections needed to realize and manifest their desires and goals. Whether it's the loop of business, the loop of high society, the loop of the artistic world in its many varied forms, the loop of government - the Eight Performance is there. The energy flow of the loop is its lifeblood.

The Lemniscate Eight Loop

Positive Pole [+]      [-] Negative Pole

However, not everything connects under the Eight vibration. As things can connect, they can disconnect as well. This disconnection characteristic is the natural opposing polarity of the connective attribute of the Eight. As we recall, all numbers have a positive and negative charge within themselves. The negative disconnective aspect of the Eight is why people under this vibration can be just as disconnective in their personalities and behavior as those who are quite noticeably connective and successful.

Success and failure are opposing poles of the same continuum, opposite sides of the same coin, opposite ends of the teeter-totter. Therefore, the Eight Performance may create success - actions which connect, integrate and interact, as well as create failure - actions which disconnect, disintegrate and are non-interactive, if not inhibitive and even destructive. This explains why some people under the Eight are successful with money, personal relationships and financial management and others are not. In the latter case, such inefficient use of money and an inability to maintain relationships may be exacerbated by a lack of Hs, Qs and Zs in the natal name (the Expression). These letters carry an Eight value numerologically and a lack of them oftentimes manifests as difficulty in the process of making and maintaining connections and integrating the flow of energy between polar extremes or between people in general. Many single people are often found missing Eights because this is the vibration which connects, and where there is no energy of connection, there is disconnection or inhibition.

Another concern with the Eight lies in the concept of negative manipulation. Because Eight seeks to connect and be successful, it may tend to do so at the expense of moral and ethical behavior, manipulating everything and everybody to get what it wants. The worldly lure of power, wealth, riches, fame, name and success, which fuels the engines of the Eight Performance, very often overpowers the individual's spiritual vision and good sense, entrapping the person in a web and loop of dishonesty, deceit, illusion, fraud, usury, misrepresentation and general untoward behavior, a spiritually tragic scenario. The Great Law of Karma -

the pure embodiment of cosmic law - brings back to everyone that which is generated and perpetrated. What we sow, we reap. Poisonous seeds bear only poisonous fruit while nourishing seeds bear life-giving nourishing fruit. Manipulation for personal gain, therefore, only spells trouble for the manipulator. He may be successful in the short run, but his negative karma will catch up to him eventually. It is interesting to note that the word "karma" is itself an Eight.

```
K   A   R   M   A
2   1   9   4   1   =   17   >   1 + 7   =   8
```

The Eight Performance would best be served to focus on making positive connections which yield positive results for itself and others. Eights need to be the 'mover'. Be the 'doer'. Be the 'connector'. Be the success-oriented person. Be the CEO, the executive, leader, manager, commander, principal, president, coordinator, but. . . do not misuse or violate the special integrative, interconnective, managerial social skills and talents inherent in the Eight energy. Walk a karmically tight line. What the Eight person does will return to him in spades. Therefore, the admonition is to play the connective game of life well, but play it honestly and ethically and never forget that, "What goes around, comes around."

The 9 Performance [PE or Role in Life]

As a Nine Performance, you manifest a power and charisma unlike any of the other eight basic vibrations. Nine is the final vibratory experience of the soul as it journeys through the numerical Avenue of Crowns - the singe digit numbers one through nine, aka, the alpha-numeric spectrum. Since Nine is the Grand Elemental, being a composite of the nine single digits, it contains all vibrations within it and, therefore, understands and identifies and is understood and identified by all (see *The King's Book of Numerology, Volume I: Foundations & Fundamentals*). Thus, Nine is the vibration of all people, the 'many', the masses, the public stage, the universal theater of man.

The Nine Performance spans many areas of life's universal theater and is, in fact, a prime vibration within the specific arena of the artistic theater, drama, radio, and television. But it is also present in the healing arts, literary arts, language arts, musical arts, metaphysical arts, martial arts and all creative and performing arts in general. Notice the word, 'Art'. Nine is definitely artistic and it is no accident that it spans all cultures, all races, all geographical, financial, social, ethnic, environmental and governmental boundaries.

The Nine Performance maintains an expanded focus, often national, international and global in dimension. As a Nine Performance, you are a person for all people because you understand all people and people consciously or subconsciously identify with you. You have a natural charisma that radiates even when you just stand still. Your vibratory essence rules. You are strong, dominant, powerful.

This natural power and strength of the Nine is one of its greatest assets. It is also one of its greatest liabilities. Although Nine dominates, it can also be domineering to its detriment. No one likes a bully or one who abuses his power, authority or position. As Lord Acton wrote in a letter to Bishop Mandell Creighton (5 April 1887), "Power tends to corrupt and absolute power corrupts absolutely." Charles Caleb Colton declares, "No man is wise enough, nor good enough to be trusted with unlimited power" (1825). Percy Shelley, the famous English poet of the Nineteenth Century, muses in Queen Mab, "Power, like a desolating pestilence, pollutes whatever it touches." This is one of the dangers of the Nine Performance: it can be corrupt, arrogant, imperious, overbearing and powerfully destructive. Therefore, Nine people need to keep a tight rein/reign on their actions.

To illustrate this principle of the abuse of power, there is a story in spiritual annals of a queen who ruled oppressively, her tyrannical nature causing much hardship, pain, suffering and anguish in the lives of her subjects, souls she was given to serve. As a result of spending her life in being a wicked and ignoble queen, in her next life God gave her the incarnation and form of a donkey, a beast of burden. Her punishment - to carry the burdens of others on her back for her entire life as she had caused others to be burdened by her when she was in the role of the ruler queen.

This is a poignant story. In the grand spiritual scope of creation, we never know what the divine purpose of our present incarnation is. Perhaps we are given the role of a ruler - a king, queen, president, prime minister, executive, magistrate, manager, law-enforcement officer, judge, etc., to determine, from a spiritual perspective, if we are capable of handling the power that comes when one is placed in such a position to ascertain our worth in receiving more and greater spiritual power. God is always testing our soundness. Worldly power may just be a test to see if we are capable of managing spiritual power. If we misuse the power associated with some little earthly position, how could we possibly be granted the responsibility of power associated with spiritual ascendance?

Regardless of the position or vibration in which our Expression is cast, we can never forget for one moment that we are accountable for everything we do, say or think and, in one way or another, at one time or another, we will pay for our abuses, our indiscretions, crimes, negative behaviors and untoward actions. Karmic Law is inviolable and infinitely more powerful than any of the Nine basic vibrations including the Nine. Thus, it is always important to take the high road but the low ground, especially if we, doing this life, walk in the cloak and carry the scepter of the Nine Performance. Nine rules, but it may rule to its detriment and, if not careful, guarantee, by its abuse of power, future lives and incarnations of oppressive personal slavery in the form of a donkey perhaps, as our previous story illustrates, or even in other ways as Karmic Law dictates. Therefore, Nines, be wise. Rule well. Your actions will become your executioner or liberator.

As the Six expression loves personally, the Nine Performance loves impersonally. Its focus is on the masses, not the solitary individual, save the fact that each person is a part of the great whole. Nine is not a domestic energy. It is a public, universal energy. It moves on the public stage of life, its true and natural home.

When its energy rises to its highest level, the Nine Performance is the humanitarian, the universal giver, the loyal, devoted, committed servant of the people and the common good.

Nine is often seen, therefore, in the charts of teachers, religious leaders, doctors, nurses, dentists, social workers, philanthropists and all types of occupations in which contact with the public is standard operating procedure. Nine touches all people, serves all people, embraces all people because it is all people.

As a Nine Performance, enjoy your charisma. Enjoy your talents. Enjoy your power and strength. Enjoy the grand stage of life. Enjoy mixing and moving among the world's many and varied peoples. Love your artistic side. Embellish your humanitarian side. Be the gracious, grand, magnanimous, generous, universal giver. This is you at your best. Rule well and remember that true rulership is based on service, not dominance; on meeting the needs of others, not satisfying your own. Teach, entertain, help, heal, uplift, serve, rule. "Only the highest can help the lowest," says Saint Charan Singh. As a Nine Performance, you hold, at least temporarily in this incarnation, an exalted position. Exalt Him. Serve Him and others and you, too, will be exalted. But. . . abuse your power and position and you, too - yes, even you, will be abused in time through the very Law that placed you where you are - Karmic Law, the Ruler in this dimension of polar opposites.

Chapter Five

THE SOUL
[Desires/Needs/Wants]

The Soul vibrations arguably play the most critical role in our love lives. They are the engine that fuels us and makes us go. They represent the fire that burns deeply within each of us; a fire, however, invisible to all except us.

The Soul energies are two: the Natural Soul [referred to as simply the Soul], which is derived from the vowels A-E-I-O-U-Y in our full name at birth (the Expression), and the Material Soul, which is the Natural Soul added to the Lifepath.

The reason the Soul couplet is so critical to our life, loves and relationships is that it describes our innermost desires, needs and wants. It comprises an aspect of our being that is not visible or known to the outside world. In other words, other people can't see our most basic desires and therefore they do not know what stirs each of us at the very core of our beings. Yet, this very private Soul couplet is arguably the most critical set of energies in a person's life and needs tending to beyond all others.

The Soul vibrations are the engine of our being. They fuel, drive and motivate us to do what we do because they represent what we most want, need, even crave from life. When our lives give us experiences matching and harmonizing with our Soul currents, i.e., when we get what we want out of life, we are potentially fulfilled and happy, some exceptions allowed. When experiences and situations run contrary or opposite to our Soul's energies, we feel, sense and experience friction, frustration, discomfort, struggle, stress, pain and sorrow. Therefore, in a very real manner the Soul energies, although the least visible of all the energies in a person's life, represent the most powerful energies in the chart.

From a love standpoint, it is important to remember that the Soul energies in both Natural and Material forms reflect what we want and desire in life. These energies must be fulfilled for us to be happy and content, at least in a worldly sense. The same thing goes for the people we most love and want to nurture. Their Soul energies must be fulfilled, too. If we know what those energies are, we can address them and work to help those we love enjoy a fulfilling and contented life. But if we neglect the Soul energies of those whom we love and don't take the time to really know them (the individual and his Soul energies), then they and we will not be as happy as we might otherwise be. Therefore, to be true lovers in the deepest and fullest sense of the word, we must ask ourselves, "What do the people I love need most to be happy and fulfilled?" Once we determine their Soul ciphers, we can then help them get what they most want out of life. When each partner in a relationship does this, the results are wonderful. It's a win/win. Each person gets what they need and want. However, if one or the other partner neglects this aspect of their partner's most intrinsic desires, the relationship will suffer accordingly. Of all the numbers in a person's numerology chart, it is the Soul numbers we would be well-served to ascertain first because they reveal the most personal secrets of what a person needs, wants, desires and craves from life. When each partner finds that need and fills it for the other, bingo! There is love and attraction.

Thus, in knowing both our own Soul energies and those with whom we are in relationship, we have solved a most critical part of the puzzle of love. Being able to satisfy the needs of both will certainly generate more fulfillment, stability, harmony and joy.

(Note: For a full assessment of both the Natural Soul and Material Soul, read *The King's Book of Numerology: Volume I - Foundations & Fundamentals*.)

Calculating the Natural Soul

To calculate the Natural Soul, simply associate the numerical value of the vowels A-E-I-O-U-Y with those in the natal name using the chart below, add left to right and reduce to a single digit.

Vowel Value Chart						
Vowels	A	E	I	O	U	Y
Values	1	5	9	6	3	7

Example #1: Mary Jane Smith: Soul

M	A	R	Y	J	A	N	E	S	M	I	T	H		
	1+		7+		1+		5+			9			=	23
23 > 2 + 3 = 5														
The Natural Soul of Mary Jane Smith is a **5**														

Example #2: John David Doey: Soul

J	O	H	N	D	A	V	I	D	D	O	E	Y		
	6+				1+		9+			6+	5+	7	=	34
34 > 3 + 4 = 7															
The Natural Soul of John David Doey is a **7**															

What's your Soul number or that of someone you love? Using the *Vowel Value Chart* below, enter the vowels of the name and their corresponding numbers, add and reduce to a single digit.

Vowel Value Chart						
Vowels	A	E	I	O	U	Y
Values	1	5	9	6	3	7

Vowels								
Values								
Add/Reduce								
Natural Soul is a _____								

Calculating the Material Soul [MS]

Calculating the Material Soul is very easy. Simply add the Soul to the Lifepath. Mary Jane Smith's Lifepath is a 7 and John David Doey's Lifepath is a 9. To find each of their Material Soul energies, we simply follow the equation and fill in the numbers.

Material Soul Calculation: Soul + Lifepath = Material Soul

1. Mary Jane Smith: Soul is 5; Lifepath is 7; Material Soul is 3.

Soul	+	Lifepath	=	Material Soul
5	+	7	=	12 > 1 + 2 = 3
Mary Jane Smith's Material Soul is a 3				
Mary's two Soul energies are a 5 and a 3				

2. John David Doey: Soul is 7; Lifepath is 9; Material Soul is 7.

Soul	+	Lifepath	=	Material Soul
7	+	9	=	16 > 1 + 6 = 7
John David Doey's Material Soul is a 7				
John's two Soul energies are both 7s				

What's your Material Soul number or that of someone you love? Using the grid below, add the Soul to the Lifepath to arrive at the Material Soul using the addition and reduction process.

Soul	+	Lifepath	=	Material Soul
	+		=	
Material Soul is a _____				
The Two Soul energies are: ____ and ____				

Now that we've calculated the Natural Soul and Material Soul numbers, let's take a look at what they represent - our most basic desires, needs, wants and motivations. Keep in mind that each person will have two different Soul energies except for a person with a 9 Lifepath. Both Soul energies are valid and need to be addressed. The Natural Soul is the most primal of the two and represents our purest desires. The Material Soul represents our desires as they relate to this material world; hence, its label.

Soul Descriptions

Soul Energy: 1

A One [1] Soul cipher means that your primary motivations are in the realm of the self and its sense of independence, leadership, achievement, accomplishment, creativity, fulfillment and personal satisfaction. One is the masculine energy of the Life

Polarity Matrix, the 'yang' of the ancient Tao. It is the vibration of personal drive, action, creativity, assertion, dominance, will, leadership, independence, self-reliance. One's go first and show the way. They like to be either in the lead or in the center of life's circumstances. They do not like to serve others or take a back seat to anyone or anything. Therefore, at heart you are the lone wolf, the maverick, the one set apart. Regardless of what your destiny may choose for you, you definitely desire not to be a hand-holder or a person dependent on others. You like to go first, be the leader, the center of attention, the star. You are the one who wants to make the decisions. Just keep in mind that just as the earth moves around the sun, so you move around the Sun of Spirit. God is at the root of your intense individuality. If you want to avoid trouble, make sure your ego subordinates itself to Him or He will relieve you of your special status.

One is a fire sign. Therefore, it is dynamic. As a One Soul, therefore, your deepest desires are dynamically aglow, if not aflame. You are the supreme "doer" of the alpha-numeric spectrum. You have vision. You also have a sense of pioneering, of doing what others cannot or will not do. You want to be active, not passive, igniting the flame of life in others.

Your One Soul may make you deeply creative, especially with words, causing you to create using language as your canvass You may also have a strong desire to be the head of the family or a primary mover in the work environment. Depending on the root structure of the single cipher [see *The King's Book of Numerology, Volume I: Foundations & Fundamentals*], you may desire to be a leader in the business and commercial fields; an entrepreneur, your own boss, your own decision maker. Leading the way as a humanitarian is also probable. Regardless of exactly how the One will play itself out, you definitely desire to be your own person and do things your way because your independent spirit knows it can get the job done and take responsibility for its actions.

As a One Soul, you must guard against being too self-absorbed, self-centered, self-consumed. There are other Ones, other people, in the world, and although they may not be driven to be as independent as you, as leadership-oriented as you, as creative, assertive and active as you, nonetheless, they are God's children, too, deserving of respect and attention, no less than you. It is the pure One who is one with all and one with the ONE. Such a state demands the utmost humility and divine understanding. Let this be the guide to your purest desires, wants and needs.

<u>Soul Energy: 2</u>

With a 2 in your Soul, your basic desires, wants and needs rest in the field of relationships and others. You are one who endeavors to harmonize situations, bringing peace, equilibrium and balance to the ever undulating, if not conflicting, ebbing and flowing of life's polarized energies. In simpler words, you are a peace-maker, a diplomat at heart. You are not generally aggressive but passive and responsive. You have a need to support and care for others. Your Two Soul represents the female principle of the universe, the 'yin' of the Life Polarity Matrix. This does not make you effeminate, although it may enhance a woman's natural Two energy.

A Two Soul generally makes you more comfortable with following rather than leading because the Two energy is quiescent by nature, not active like the male one energy, at least on the surface. It is, however, very active underneath the surface, which is why women, ruled by the number Two, have often been referred to as "the power behind the throne."

Two is a water sign. It flows. Its path is to go around things, not through them. As an expression of water, next to air - our most precious substance and nutrient, you are in a sense a nurturer. Seeds, for example, may be active and grow to produce fruit-giving trees, but they need support, they need nutrition in order to grow and flourish. As part of their nutritional requirement, seeds obviously need water to grow, some less than more, but all life needs water to develop and survive. At your deepest core, you desire to be the water which nourishes through love, caring, support, balance and equilibrium.

Your Two Soul may be activated in a desire to be competitive and dominant because Two, operating in the realm of others, rules competition and adversarial conditions. Many great athletes, competitors and lawyers have Two dominant in their charts. They like one-on-one challenges to see who the best is when pitted against each other.

Because Two rules balance, there is also a strong desire for you to be the diplomat or negotiator, the one who brings both sides of an issue or argument together and creates harmony. Again, this speaks to the peace-making aspect of the Two. Yet, the opposite side of peace is war, and depending on other aspects in your chart, you may like to create confrontation, interference and problems for others. This would be most unwise because the seeds we plant always bear fruit that we are eventually forced to eat. "As we sow, so shall we reap," is the eternal law of this creation, and it applies to everyone. No one escapes karmic law.

Two is an extremely intuitive number. Therefore, you are encouraged to use your intuition to solve problems. And because Two rules female energy, you are also enjoined to express Yin characteristics. If you are a male, know that feminine does not equate to effeminate. Being in touch with the Two [feminine] energy means to be tender-hearted, supportive, helpful, encouraging, balancing, the team player and partner, the one who bends when need be, and who understands both sides of issues.

When positively aspected, you are a great help to many people, the supporter that others need, the follower to the leader, the volunteer who gives without expectation of recognition. You may not like to be the star, the one out front of the pack, or the one who makes the final decision, but you definitely desire to be involved in helping and seeing things through to their completion. The highest expression of the Two is balance. Therefore, using your instinctive ability to create balance will be of great service to everyone.

Soul Energy: 3

Your 3 Soul energy is focused in the field of self-expression, communication, health, words, writing, singing, image, beauty. This need may manifest in a desire to be an actor, singer, writer, model, lawyer or artist of any genre. With this Three Soul, it is intrinsically natural for you to want to seek joy, pleasure, ease and good times and share these with those in your world. You have a need to integrate, whether socially, artistically, economically, lovingly, mentally, sexually or spiritually. You love beauty and that which is perfect by design. At their highest levels, these desires may well express themselves in a divine capacity where being in touch with God and the Trinity is of vital importance.

A Three Soul often creates a desire and need to sing - the process of vocally combining the qualities of love with harmony, rhythm and words in an expressive capacity. It may also manifest in desires to be on the public stage and in the universal theater as an actor, actress, newscaster, journalist, reporter. Because Three governs beauty and image, you may desire to be a photographer or model. In fact, many world-class models have Three dominant in their charts.

Three rules health and well-being. Therefore, to be involved in the health and wellness aspect of life may well be an important part of your basic needs.

Three rules children. Having a need to positively influence the youth of the world may be a strong desire in you. After all, in all cultures children are its future, and the more whole children are, the greater the potential outcome in creating a whole society.

One of the considerations of the Three Soul is the difference in the pleasure it seeks. On an earthly level, the Three will seek, want, need and desire material and sensual comfort and human companionship. On a spiritual level, the Three will seek to express the divine beauty and perfection in all things of the Spirit. Three represents perfection and is the sign of the Trinity: Father-Son-Holy Ghost; Master-Disciple-Word; Man-Woman-Marriage;

Father-Mother-Child. Three also integrates these three separate components into one, unified, spiritual whole.

On a cautionary note, because Three rules pleasure, it would be wise to control your pleasure-seeking side. Three can elevate people to wonderfully fulfilling heights, but be warned: no number has destroyed more people than the Three running out of control with reckless abandon, thoughtless of its well-being, its future and the joy and happiness of others.

Pleasures such as recreational drug use, alcohol consumption, illicit sex, partying too much and basically being blind to the fact that the opposite side of pleasure is pain can create a mountain range of problems, far more problems than the pleasure is worth. Show business, as one example, has produced a tragic litany of actors, actresses, singers and celebrities who have over-indulged in the pleasures of the senses to their ultimate demise, let alone their health. This should serve as a sobering warning, especially for those who seek a joyous and healthy life. It's appropriate here to repeat the words of Saint Charan Singh: *No matter how great the pleasures of the world may be, they are not only short lived but also have equally unpleasant reactions at some time or another.* Another Saint, Ravidas, stated: *True happiness lies in realizing true holiness.* Holiness equates to purity of living. Thus, the purer the living, the greater the potential for true happiness.

Soul Energy: 4

As a Four Soul, your needs, wants and desires are centered in concepts and principles of stability, security, strength, roots, work, unchanging regularity, convention, tradition, construction and social movement. The Four, like all basic numbers, possesses different root forms which color its desires, giving it different sets of clothes so to speak, [see *The King's Book of Numerology, Volume I: Foundations & Fundamentals*] but in a general sense, all people with a Four Soul love to be stable and secure. They do not want change to disrupt their lives and leave them feeling insecure - financially, emotionally, physically, psychologically, structurally, domestically.

As a Four Soul, you love roots, the bigger, stronger and deeper the better. You like anchors too, and may even like being the anchor that weathers all storms. Fours are generally conventional, not choosing to wander out of the boundaries which give them the security they seek. In fact, they usually spend a great deal of energy creating boundaries and secure systems to give them the comfort they need. Many very wealthy people have Four Souls because money buys them the security and stability they desire, at least from a worldly perspective.

A Four Soul generally wants to build and construct - anything from actual buildings and material structures to financial portfolios and integrated families. The Four also enjoys serving and doing for others, especially were the focus is on order and organization. Librarians often have Four in their charts and they are some of the most ardent servants in the public service environment. It's quite common to find Certified Public Accountants [CPAs] expressing Four energy. Sculptors, whose art involves working in the realm of form, often reflect Four ciphers in their charts. Body builders, carpenters, mechanics, secretaries, personal assistants and law enforcement personnel are some other types of people who often have Four energy in their charts. The common thread - order and service.

Four Soul people enjoy working and are not afraid to work. They also tend to "go with the flow," not wanting to upset the status quo. They are quite strong individuals, and seem to weather the storms of life better than any other number.

One of the cautions of the Four Soul individual is to not allow stability to become rigidity. Roots are fine, but if those roots inordinately attach you to some idea, concept, opinion, place, person etc., you may find yourself too anchored to move and change when it's expedient to do so in order to survive. History is replete with people who have lost their lives stubbornly defending their property, for example, in the onslaught of a hurricane or other natural disaster when it would have been prudent for them to move to a safer place. One's life is more important than one's opinion, position or possessions. The moral of the story: if you cast an anchor into the seas of life, make sure you can pull it up when you need to. Be flexible and open to change. It may change your life for the better.

Soul Energy: 5

As a Five Soul, your needs, desires and wants are focused in principles and concepts of freedom, detachment, change, speed, fun, motion, movement, variety, diversity, people, experience, adventure, exploration, unconventionality, sex and the senses. Unlike the Four, you do not crave that which is conventional, traditional, stagnant, unmoving and arguably boring. You like and need excitement, change and freedom to make you content. This need will cause your mind to explore new things, to break the bonds of convention, or at least step outside them to experience what it is like outside the fences or walls of normal convention, custom, practice, procedure, fashion, routine and staid tradition.

As a Five Soul, you dream of flying, of being free to experience all you can in life. You do not like being tied down as a general rule, and if your life is fully replete with Four energy in your Lifepath or Performance, your life might seem very restrictive and confining, causing you stress or distress and discomfort. Be cautious, however, in understanding that true freedom is based in detachment from all that is not God-centered, rather than the unrestrained action and behavior normally interpreted as freedom but which can become incarcerating and enslaving. All actions do have consequences. Acting on whims of adventure and irresponsibility without regard for their consequences can create dire, painful and sometimes life-long conditions of irreversible sorrow. Being free is not being careless and irresponsible. Think before you act; i.e., think of the consequences of every behavior before it is taken. There is no such thing as action without consequence. Wisdom demands forethought.

Five Soul individuals love good times and pleasure-seeking experiences with friends. If ever there were a party vibration, this is an excellent candidate. One must be careful here because unrestrained action can generate inextricable bondage. Discipline and true understanding are vital to maintaining balance, harmony and peace with the Five energy. Where there is little or no self-control, life becomes extremely problematic. How many people have died because some fun-loving, party-minded person got drunk, jumped in a car and killed people while he or she was under the influence of alcohol? How many people have been tragically hooked on drugs because they thought it would be fun to experiment with them? How many sexually transmitted diseases have negatively impacted people's lives due to a lack of discretion and self-control? How many unwanted babies have been born after an episode of fun and frolic? Life is hard enough if we do everything right. Taking risks, which the Five loves to do, has consequences, and not all consequences are good. It is wise, therefore, to heed the words of Pythagoras: *No man is free who cannot control himself.* If the Five Soul person truly wants freedom, he or she must exercise extreme discipline and control over the senses and passions.

Once under control, however, the Five Soul person is driven to enjoy a diverse life, full of fun, new adventures and experiences. No number expresses more diversity than the Five. It is the fulcrum of the Avenue of Crowns [the single numbers One through Nine]. When tamed, the Five is more free, fun, exciting and spontaneous than any other number. If not tamed, it's like being on a runaway horse, a speed boat without a rudder and a car that's lost its steering. Therefore, the Five must never forget that one side of the Five coin is total and complete freedom, but the other side is total and compete slavery. Choose.

Soul Energy: 6

The basic needs, wants and desires of a Six Soul are centered in concepts and principles of love, nurturing, the home, domestic environment, relationships, romance, family, community, art, beauty, harmony, music, singing, and personal compassion. Six rules the heart more than any other single vibration. As a Six Soul, therefore, there is a great need for you to be personally loving and share one's life experiences with others on a personal level, a level of home and community. Sixes love the family and desire to be domestically oriented or romantically involved. None of the other numbers is as home-oriented as the Six.

All things being equal, one with this Six soul energy would be a likely candidate to be the loving mother, father, grandmother, grandfather, aunt, uncle, brother or sister. The Six is the one who offers a big hug, a warm knee to sit on or a kind ear to hear other's troubles. Cookies in the cookie jar and soft kisses for the little boo-boos of life are standard reflections of the Six energy.

Six, like the Three and Nine, is an extremely artistic energy. It is not uncommon for the Six to be prevalent in the charts of singers, musicians, actors, beauticians, interior designers, landscapers, architects, community organizers and basically any occupation in which the home and community are involved.

Because Six is personally compassionate, nurturing and tender-hearted, a desire to be a doctor, nurse, teacher, educator, counselor, or other occupation where the personal touch is important is also a viable option.

Sometimes, however, those who love love too much, and if they're not cautious, can be used and taken advantage of by people who prey on their nurturing instincts. Therefore, it's important that the Six Soul individual value his or her own worth and not become a doormat for those whose callous mindsets abuse the gifts of this personally loving individual.

As the Six is double the Three energy of pleasure, the same caution remains in effect for the Six. Misuse of drugs, sex, alcohol and other intoxicants poses as a harbinger of future problems. In consideration of such things, the words of Saint Dadu should warrant our appraisal: *Hold pure, stay pure, say pure, take the pure, give the pure.*

Soul Energy: 7

Congratulations! Your Seven Soul has placed you at the threshold of the divine! This soul vibration is like no other and is, in fact, so opposite to the ways of the world that you might find yourself feeling very isolated, alone, separate and distant from others and the general earthly status quo. People do not often understand you. You like to be alone, separate and apart, and this makes you appear cold and aloof. The irony is that you are neither cold nor aloof - maybe from the world and society, yes, but not from the deep and mystical core of all that is eternal, spiritual and divine. Your desires carry you deeply into feelings where others only touch them superficially, and while others exist on the surface of the water, you live deeply within the inner currents and tides of life, seeking causes, not effects and asking questions regarding how, why, what, when and where, for yours is the mind that never stops asking, never stops inquiring, never stops seeking answers to that which is normally held to be unknown and unknowable. But it is axiomatic that unless we seek, we can never find, and so the Seven mind is always on the proverbial treasure hunt.

It is not easy to be a Seven Soul in this world because of all the numbers in the Avenue of Crowns, it is the most internal, the most inward seeking. Contrarily, the world lives and thrives in the great 'without' and could care less about the spiritual, inner side of life.

Seven is, at its zenith, consumed with mysticism, not money. It seeks knowledge, answers to life's questions, soul liberation and salvation, not worldly success or material accumulation. The Seven Soul is the key to the inner worlds where energy, not matter, reigns supreme; where God awaits to embrace the weary and worldly lovelorn soul and take it Home to the supernal, ethereal realms of eternal peace, love, light and bliss.

As the indwelling Seven energy separates you from the external show of the phenomenal world, do not be too disconcerted. The world does not have the answers to creation. The answers exist within, not without. Your sense of and desire for isolation, withdrawal and privacy are the keys which allow you the space to go within during this critical time of the human experience where time is fleeting and few know what awaits them beyond the gates of death. Now is the time for spiritual, not worldly, progress and success. Let the world go its way. As a Seven Soul, make sure you go yours - deep within the recesses of your mind and consciousness to that place where you realize God is Real and Eternal, where you also understand that your soul can escape from this labyrinthine nightmare of restricting, sensual, ephemeral, incarcerating phenomena. Embrace the isolation and loneliness you feel. It is designed to motivate you to move beyond this world and gain your rightful heritage as a divine child of the Light, the Light which glows resplendently and eternally within.

This prior description of the Seven Soul may seem too focused on its spiritual aspects. For those who have Seven Souls and are not spiritually disposed, the potential still exists to tune in to the Seven's higher energies. If they are not desired, the more mundane characteristics of the Seven will focus on mental traits such as analysis, research, study, teaching, philosophy, writing.

One of the important things for those who love people with a Seven Soul is to understand that the Seven loves its privacy, solitude, separation. Depending on the amount of Seven energy in a chart, Sevens will need time alone - sometimes a lot of time or a little time, but still time to themselves. It's in the silence and separation that the Seven recharges and renews itself, unlike the Eight, for example, that is reinvigorated by social gatherings and group activities. Sevens are true loners, more than any other single number. They tend to be reclusive, shy, detached, withdrawn, secretive. That doesn't mean they're weird. It just means they prefer to be alone and separate. To them, isolation is an integral aspect of their life. They need it, and will not be happy unless they get it. Therefore, the way to love a Seven Soul is to give them their space and distance from time to time and not pressure them to be something they are not, social butterflies. That distinction is left to the Eight.

Soul Energy: 8

The Eight Soul desires connection and integration. Eight, the highest expression of the social numbers 2-4-6-8, loves to be in the flow of all that is happening, for Eight is the vibration that connects polar opposites manifested in life as buyer and seller, idea and completion, producer and consumer, actor and audience, directives and their execution, and so forth. Eight brings things together, makes them efficient, coordinated, successful. Eight wants to be 'in the loop' of success in any field - business/commerce, athletics, theater, politics, art, education, management and administration.

The Lemniscate Eight Loop

Positive Pole [+]      [-] Negative Pole

The Eight Soul, unlike the Seven soul, does not seek isolation or reclusion but external connection and social integration. Eight is an even number and therefore social by nature. It loves to mix and socialize unless effected by substantial Seven energy elsewhere in the chart. Therefore, Eight is a vibration common to all that is on the 'outside'. To be worldly successful is normal for this vibration.

The Eight Soul is, generally speaking, driven to seek success, wealth, fame, riches, material comfort and power in the external world of society. The caution here is to not let the desire for such earthly and temporal success overshadow the spiritually obligatory directive for moral and ethical behavior. Eight, because it loves to connect, may seek to connect through dishonest and untoward means, thus causing it much heartache at some future time when the rebounding karma of its original action returns to bless the giver with the gift - the gift of pleasure or pain, success or failure. Because of this connection-seeking quality, Eight can be an extremely manipulative vibration for better or for worse. The admonishment once again: be careful of violating karmic law. This is the vibration that returns all things to its creator. . . all things - good or bad, and if it's 'bad in', it's 'bad out'; if it's 'good in', then it's 'good out.' This is the operational law of the universe.

It's very common to see executives, generals, admirals, presidents, prime ministers and other leaders with Eight dominate in their charts and often in their Soul position. Eight is a double Four. Four rules order, organization, rules, discipline, consistency. But Four doesn't manage. It serves as the helper. It is the Eight that takes the concept of order, rules, structure, etc., and applies it to the integrative social loop as a manager and administrator where it brings people, ideas, concepts, buyers and sellers together to function smoothly in the world of business and commerce.

As an Eight Soul, you will definitely love to connect, integrate, manage, administrate, socialize and connect the dots of the social scene. You most probably love to be 'in the loop' of all that's happening in your world. In fact, you're probably the one who created the loop, the network of social participation. The number ruling socialites more than any number is the Eight. Not only does it like to mix and mingle, but if it has the resources, it can be very charitable.

Eights love to coordinate and orchestrate too. They make excellent planners and organizers of functions such as business meetings, weddings, graduations, group parties, neighborhood functions - anything that needs a person in charge to make things run smoothly and efficiently.

Another avenue for release of the Eight Soul is through understanding varying systems of mechanics, electricity, plumbing, etc. Eight governs circulation, and therefore people with an Eight Soul often love to see how things fit together, work together, flow together. Regardless of the application, the general desire of the Eight Soul is to connect and create a smooth flow to all they touch. What they touch may be money and finances, organizational development, educational systems, athletics, mechanics, character depiction [as in the case of actors], coaches, hospital administrators, etc. The key phrase is: Eights administrate, circulate, integrate, orchestrate and manipulate.

Soul Energy: 9

The Nine Soul seeks the macrocosm, the universal stage of life, the international/global landscape, the public domain, the theater of 'the many', the field of art, humanity, education and philanthropy.

Because Nine is the Grand Elemental, the Nine Soul often seeks power, rulership, dominion, completeness, completion, victory and triumph. Nine is intrinsically powerful and generally wants to dominate. The caution is that it must not be overly dominating, arrogant or imperious in the process or it will make a mockery of its higher expression of regal rulership, generosity and magnanimity.

The Nine Soul often desires to live and breathe in the arena of humanity, serving as a teacher, doctor, counselor, nurse, lawyer, theologian, humanitarian, philanthropist, artist, thespian, musician, volunteer, etc. Nine is a very complete vibration, the most complete in fact, and wants to share itself and its talents with others, assisting and helping them in whatever way it can.

Because of its connection with the macrocosm, the Nine Soul can be very ambitious. The symbol for the Nine is the crown, and the Nine Soul wants to rule, without question; not necessarily lead, but rule. There's a difference. Nines love their thrones but not so much the barren frontier.

Because of its all-encompassing nature, the Nine Soul likes to be among the many, to be recognized, publically known and famous. It is very different from the Seven which seeks its solitude. The masses, the masses - this is what the Nine Soul loves, seeks, needs and desires.

The Six energy is the most personally loving of all the numbers. The Nine is the most impersonally loving of all the numbers, but still loving. It desires to be the compassionate humanitarian and philanthropist, the giver and benefactor of all - that is unless it is negatively aspected, in which case it seeks to be the malefic, evil ruler of its subjects. Nines love to rule. They may be the benevolent ruler or the malevolent dictator. Rulership is rulership. Kings are kings. Queens are queens. Titles confer no goodness, just position.

Besides becoming too overbearing and imperious, a main caution is for the Nine Soul to be judicious in choosing the company it keeps. We become known by the company we run with, and because the Nine is the chameleon of the alpha-numeric spectrum, it can blend and mix equally well with the forces of light or darkness. Once again, rulership guarantees no inherent goodness. History teaches us that. How many powerful leaders were unwholesome leaders, to say the least?

The best advice and warning for the Nine Soul can be found in the following quotes. Thoughts for contemplation.

> *Power tends to corrupt, and absolute power corrupts absolutely. Great men are almost always bad men.*
> ~ Lord Acton

> *No man is wise enough, nor good enough to be trusted with unlimited power.* ~ Charles Caleb Colton

> *Power, like a desolating pestilence, pollutes whatever it touches.* ~ Percy Shelley

Chapter Six

THE NATURE
[The Personality]

As the Soul vibrations are derived from the vowels in the name, the Nature is derived from the consonants. The Nature, like the Soul, has two parts: Natural and Material. The Natural Nature is simply referred to as the Nature. The Material Nature, like the Material Soul, is determined by simply adding the Natural Nature to the Lifepath. Each aspect of the Nature - the Natural and Material forms - is fully discussed in *The King's Book of Numerology, Volume I: Foundations & Fundamentals.*

The Nature component [in both of its parts] describes our basic tendencies and personality. It can also be perceived as the way or manner in which we do things.

For example, assume a person has a Two Expression. This would make him or her a person who is basically supportive and passive, a team player. Yet, let's assume this Two Expression individual maintained a Nine Nature. Nine is a powerful, dominant, often charismatic vibration.

One who retains a Nine Nature would be a dominant figure, if not dominating. Remember, Nines love power. The 'way' or 'manner' such a person would behave with this Nine Nature vibration could possibly be anything but totally passive, sweet and harmonious. Nines like to rule so this combination would make for a strong supporter or, on the negative side, one who is potentially and powerfully divisive in relationships, contrary, argumentative and interfering.

If one were to consider the two aspects comprising the Expression - the Soul and the Nature - as a manifestation of the Yin and Yang, the Soul could be argued to be the passive, feminine aspect while the Nature would be the masculine, active aspect for, certainly, the Nature is an active vibration addressing the manner or way in which the Expression manifests itself.

Unlike the Soul, whose energies are hidden from view, the Nature is quite visible. We can't hide how we behave. We are who we are, and the Nature is a major component putting us on public display.

Calculating the Nature

To calculate the Nature, simply associate the numerical value of the consonants with those in the natal name, add left to right and reduce to a single digit. We'll use our friends, Mary Jane Smith and John David Doey. For easy reference, here's the letter value chart again:

	Simple Letter Value Chart							
The Letters	A	B	C	D	E	F	G	H	I
	J	K	L	M	N	O	P	Q	R
	S	T	U	V	W	X	Y	Z	
Number Value	1	2	3	4	5	6	7	8	9

Example #1: Mary Jane Smith: Nature

M	A	R	Y	J	A	N	E	S	M	I	T	H		
4+		9+		1+		5+		1+	4+		2+	8	=	34

34 > 3 + 4 = 7
The Nature of Mary Jane Smith is a 7

Mary's Nature is a 7. Here's a quick way to check our work. Since we already know from our previous study that Mary's Expression is a 3 [calculated from all the letters in her name, both vowels and consonants] and her Soul is a 5 [calculated from the vowels], the remaining consonants must add up to a 7.

Quick Check Formula: Mary

Vowels	+	Consonants	=	Expression
Soul	+	Nature	=	Expression
5	+	?	=	3
5	+	7	=	12 > 1+2 = 3

If we had wanted, we could have simply determined the Nature using this Quick Check Formula by filling in the missing number. When we know any two of the numbers in the formula, the third is easy to determine.

Example #2: John David Doey: Nature

J	O	H	N	D	A	V	I	D	D	O	E	Y		
1+	8+	5+	4+			4+		4+	4				=	30

30 > 3 + 0 = 1
The Nature of John David Doey is a 3

John's Expression is a 1. His Soul is a 7. Therefore, he would have to have a 3 Nature. Let's check our work.

Quick Check Formula: John

Vowels	+	Consonants	=	Expression
Soul	+	Nature	=	Expression
7	+	?	=	1
7	+	3	=	10 > 1+0 = 0

What is your Nature or that of someone you love? To compute it, add the consonants of the natal name and reduce to a single digit, or use the Quick Check Formula.

Vowels	+	Consonants	=	Expression
Soul	+	Nature	=	Expression
#____	+	?	=	#____
____	+	____	=	____

Calculating the Material Nature [MN]

Calculating the Material Nature is very easy. Simply add the Nature to the Lifepath. Mary's Lifepath is a 7 and John's Lifepath is a 9. Let's see what their Material Natures are.

Material Nature Calculation: Nature + Lifepath = MN

1. Mary Jane Smith: Nature is 7; LP is 7; Material Nature is 5.

Nature	+	Lifepath	=	Material Nature
7	+	7	=	14 > 1 + 4 = 5
Mary Jane Smith's Material Nature is a 5				

2. John David Doey: Nature is 3; LP is 9; Material Nature is 3.

Nature	+	Lifepath	=	Material Nature
3	+	9	=	12 > 1 + 2 = 3
John David Doey's Material Nature is a 3.				

What's your Material Nature or that of your loved one?

Nature	+	Lifepath	=	Material Nature
	+		=	
Material Nature is a _____				

Following are the Nature descriptions. One explanation will suffice for both. It may be helpful to review the Expression, PE and Soul descriptions for each number as well to increase the understanding of each number.

Nature Descriptions

Nature Energy: 1

With One in the Nature or Material Nature position, the way or manner in which you do things is centered in the 'yang' aspect of the Life. This, of course, represents the male energy manifested as self, ego, will, action, initiation, creation, courage, independence, assertiveness, leadership. You are a self-starter and like to be in the lead or in the center. You are creative and assertive, love to do things your own way. You tend to be driven from within yourself, not driven by others. You like to stand alone and be seen as your own person, replete with your own ideas, values and sense of being. You also tend to be logical and reasonable rather than illogical and emotional. You behave in a direct manner, not indirect. In other words, you prefer face-to-face interaction rather than employing a third party to do your talking or bidding for you.

One is a fire sign and since it is the substance of your One Nature, you can heat things up. Fire is active and so are you - driving, pushing, leading, creating, manifesting, doing. You can easily be seen, not just as the leader, but as the mother or father figure. You like to go first and show the way. In two words, you lead.

One of the cautions of your One Nature is the over-assertiveness of your ego and pride. Be careful here. Ones can become too self-centered, too self-absorbed, too ego-centric, too arrogant, too aggressive, oftentimes for their own good. Ones do not like to follow others. They like to go before others or be the center of attention where other ones focus on them. They do this because they know they can get the job done. Ones like to initiate and get things moving. They do not like to wait around.

Ones also do not like to bend. They can be very rigid. Sometimes this can be very beneficial, especially when strong, decisive leadership is required. Sometimes, however, a softer approach may be the best solution. Kind words and honey go a long way in influencing others and motivating them, as opposed to iron wills and hands. Leadership is all about balance and knowing when to apply the proper touch at the proper time. Sometimes a kind word is needed. Other times a pat on the back or an arm around the shoulder works magic. Then again, like an alpha mare or a stallion, a good swift kick is the solution.

When Ones understand their oneness with the universe and place themselves in the proper perspective as a solitary, short-lived, single bubble on the great cosmic ocean of life, they can become truly radiant and divine. We all need leaders and creators but ones which, like a branch hung heavy with fruit, bow low to the ground and share their wonderful gift, substance and nourishment with others.

Nature Energy: 2

With Two in the Nature or Material Nature position the way or manner in which you do things is centered in the 'yin' or female aspect of the Life. Thus, as you work to the highest level of the Two energy, you are warm, supportive, caring, congenial, cooperative, conciliatory, cordial, comprising, compassionate, diplomatic, pleasant, agreeable, friendly, gentle, kind-hearted, emotional, considerate, inspirational and partnership oriented.

You are prone to being a soft touch. Your gentle nature draws others to you as well as your tactful sense of dealing with situations and people. You like to help, support and assist others and prefer being more passive than overly assertive or aggressive. Your nature is not seen as one who is self-centered, dominant or hungry for leadership or the spotlight. You are more comfortable in the background in a support role. You would prefer to be the "power behind the throne" than the one sitting on the throne; the one behind the camera, not in front of it. Rather than create turmoil or disturbance as some people like to do, you prefer to be the peacemaker and healer of discord. Equilibrium, balance and peace are important to you. Your gentle way of being and manner of behaving act as a salve, soothing the ills and heartaches of others.

However, as everything in the universe possesses a negative charge, especially numerical vibrations, the Two does have its dark side. One of the characteristics of the nether pole of the Two lies in its duality and duplicity. Two can be as openly discordant as it is concordant, as truculent and warlike as it is peaceful, as contentious as it is conciliatory. Of the ten binary roots forming its 2 single-ciphered crown (11-20-29-38-47-56-65-74-83-92), all but the Twenty intrinsically carry an Eleven transition root (see *The King's Book of Numerology, Volume I: Foundations & Fundamentals*). As you'll notice, except for the number 20, when the single numbers of each of the Two's binary roots are added together, an 11 emerges in the reduction process [29 > 2 + 9 = 11; 38 > 3 + 8 = 11, etc. This 11 is called a transition root. All single digits have a binary root structure.

Eleven (11) is a high intensity master number juxtaposing dual Ones, Ones which often exist in opposition to one another. These dual Ones can be seen as one person versus another person; one system of ideals versus another system of ideals; one religious philosophy versus another religious philosophy. This juxtaposition of Ones often manifests as competition, contention, opposition, conflict, hostility, resistance and a general adversarial relationship between people, ideals, concepts. Because Two rules others and relationships as well as duality, this can create obvious problems. War is the polar opposite of peace. Since both war and peace constitute the polar apexes of the Two continuum, there is as much a possibility of one charge being manifested as the other. Thus, a

Two Nature in its lowest level of expression can be extremely combative, aggressive, hostile and militant, creating disharmony, discord, disruption, contention, strife, competition, disputation, opposition and antagonism. Yet, the Eleven master number can also be extremely inspirational and encouraging, helping others realize their goals and dreams - if its operating at its highest level.

The key for the Two Nature is to strive to express the positive energy of the Two. Unlike the uncontrollable events and circumstances of our lives, we do have the ability to choose how we act and react to life's events. Markedly, this is especially true for the Two because it is intrinsically dual by nature and, hence, is the vibration manifesting the true life test of balance and equilibrium. Therefore, as a Two Nature your challenge is to find the golden mean, the middle ground between polar opposites and manifest it. See both sides. Be diplomatic. Be balancing and. . . be at peace.

Nature Energy: 3

With Three in the Nature or Material Nature, your way and manner of doing things revolve around that which is pleasant, expressive, communicative. You are one of the easiest and friendliest people on earth to know. You smile a great deal of the time and people love to be around you. You are very embracing and approachable. Too, it is harder for things to get you down than most of the other vibrations. This is a result of your positive attitude which always finds you seeing or seeking the silver lining in dark and foreboding situations.

If there is a social butterfly among the Avenue of Crowns, it is you, especially if there is some Eight energy in your chart. No number is more fun, social, artistic, gregarious and genuinely happy than the Three. You see just about everybody as a friend. This includes children, adults and animals alike. Your personality naturally exudes a pleasantness unlike anyone else.

As the triangle is the ancient symbol of perfection, it can be effectively argued that your nature seeks to express perfection and personal integration. Health is as natural to you as beauty. And the beauty we're talking about is not necessarily physical beauty, although that is highly possible with the Three, but internal personal beauty, the kind that emanates from the spirit and the heart. Having a religious or spiritual point of reference are also strong potentials in your character makeup.

The opposite side of the Three coin of ease, happiness, self-expression and perfection is one which reflects dis-ease, unhappiness, negative self-expression and disintegration. Not having a good self-image or too strong an image are possibilities.

The Three energy rules beauty as we mentioned, and Three people are often quite physically beautiful, even stunning. Such beauty does draw attention, lots of it. If the individual is not anchored in a sense of humility, such attention can easily grow into vanity and arrogance, a glaring narcissism in which the personality is forever shouting, "Look at me! Look at me! Look at me! Aren't I beautiful, lovely, exquisite?" Divinely speaking, only God is beautiful and He is eternal. Ephemeral beauty is a potential trap for ego-generating karma. As the mystic Rumi queried, *Don't you see how many beautiful faces are buried underneath the earth*? Therefore, a person born beautiful in this life should enjoy his or beauty but not allow it to get out of control. If that were to happen, it would not be inconceivable for the individual to be born ugly in the next life in order to bring a sense of balance to the soul. That's why the great lesson of the Three Nature is to reflect the quality of divine perfection, personally expressed as the virtue humility, not the folly of vanity.

Three loves pleasure, but it's best to seek pleasure of that which is pure and leads one to health and wholeness of the spirit. Because of the pleasure-seeking quality of the Three, there is the risk of the Three saturating itself in worldly pleasures which will only lead to enormous pain and suffering. As Saint Dadu exclaims, *Hold pure, stay pure, say pure, take the pure, give the pure.* Saint Ravidas states, *True happiness lies in realizing true holiness*, and 19th Century Mystic, Swami Ji Maharaj, corroborates, *All worldly pleasures are a source of pain and eventually will betray their possessors.*

As a Three Nature, be appreciative of the loveliness, ease and friendliness you radiate but do not misuse or abuse it. It is only a loan and a gift. Recognize the divine beauty in all people and especially recognize the Source from which all beauty and loveliness spring. . . God Himself.

Nature Energy: 4

With Four in the Nature or Material Nature, your way and manner of doing things are the most structured of all the basic numbers. Unless offset by a strong contingent of Five energy in your chart, you are relentless in your pursuit to have things remain stable, secure, confined, conventional and traditional. At its most positive point, this Four Nature is manifested as the loyal, devoted, diligent worker, friend, associate and employee, steadfast in upholding company policy and serving the employer with responsibility, reliability, dependability and trustworthiness.

Four is the vibration of roots, anchors and solid, immovable rocks. Four seldom budges. It sinks its teeth into its work and sticks right to the task. It is diligent, dogged and dependable.

Fours can go on forever without change. They like routine. Keeping things just the same is intrinsic to them. They do not like to move, adjust or be displaced. They love security and would much rather stay at home than explore the outer reaches of Never-Never Land. The Four Nature is strong, unbending, untiring, unwavering, service-oriented and relentless. Four is the vibration of discipline, control, persistence, perseverance and commonalty.

As a Four Nature, you are practical, pragmatic, orderly, sensible and systematic. You need to be these things to ensure your security, stability and safety. You are not a risk-taker in general; nor are you very spontaneous. To get up and go on a moment's notice just on a lark to fly upon the wind to see where it will take you is not you. It's frankly too risky for you. But you are an excellent servant in the greatest sense of the word. And you can be an excellent builder of things, concepts and ideas.

The negative side of the Four Nature is that it can be too rigid for its own good. Fours can sometimes be so stubborn and unyielding they refuse to make sensible adjustments and critically positive changes. This rigidity can cause them to be blind to new, different and better ways of thinking, acting and doing. Progress, however, is based on change and the shedding of old skin, of old and outdated habits, ideals, patterns and entrenched ideas and concepts; in rounding out and softening the edges of the square of your basic nature so it's not too abrasive to others.

Although being rock-solid and immovable can be virtuous, given the right set of circumstances, it can also be deadly. This is one critical aspect of the Four - it doesn't always move, adjust and change when, perhaps, it would be better served to do so.

As Four is the vibration of building and construction, it is also the vibration of destruction - its negative polarity, the other side of the Four coin. The universe expands and contracts. Just as there is life, there is death. Physical structures such as buildings and mountains, as well as social structures such as empires, rise and fall. Such is the nature of life. Your Four Nature expresses both. How you choose to express it is germane to your well-being.

All in all, as a Four Nature you are the rock of the Avenue of Crowns, the salt of the earth, the anchor in the storm. Your beauty rests in your commitment to the ideals of strength, courage, devotion, control, service, security, dependability, fidelity, loyalty, hard work, persistence and undaunted determination. People trust you, a gift that should never be taken for granted, for it is trust that is the basis of all lasting relationships, and when the glass of trust is shattered it can never be, like Humpty-Dumpty, put back together again.

Nature Energy: 5

With Five in the Nature or Material Nature, your way and manner of doing things focus on issues involving freedom, movement, motion, exploration, experience, adventure, detachment and change. You like variety and enjoy being non-conventional. You do not like to stay in one place as a rule because you get bored. This may be offset by a Four Soul, Expression, Lifepath or Performance-Experience energy which would make you more stable and create conflict with your Five Nature which does not like to be tied down. Fours and Fives are direct opposites.

You are also more sensual than many of the other natures because Five rules the five senses. You also like to be around people, different kinds of people, for they stimulate your need to explore and experience. You like to talk and converse and would do well in situations where you are free to move about, unrestricted by the conventions which others find comfortable and traditional.

All Fives love freedom and this is where you must be careful with your mercurial nature. Freedom, true freedom, is the result of great discipline, restraint and self-control. True freedom is based solidly in the concept of detachment. Too often, freedom is defined as action without consequence, but the reality of life is that all actions produce consequences and too much uninhibited action devoid of the consideration of consequence or an appropriate amount of critical thinking, can produce horrendously negative results. Freedom, for example, does not equate to unlicensed, wanton sensual indulgence or promiscuity. And if any number has a reputation for being wild, indulgent, promiscuous and a party animal, it is the Five. Such unbridled actions can lead to incarcerating emotional, physical, financial, social and sexual confinement, disease, even death - hardly a condition of freedom. Life doesn't always give second chances, and a single, solitary act of miscalculation, lack of forethought, discipline and self-control, can create a lifetime of sorrow and sadness.

Yet, when responsible action is undertaken as a result of clear thinking, and forethought and discretion are used to generate appropriate restraint, pure detachment from those actions of wanton, unrestrained indulgence can lead to real freedom, liberating freedom - the state of being detached from all things which bind the soul and limit its spiritual ascent. As a Five Nature, it would be wise for you to consider this point of view. Enjoy your freedom and love of experience but be careful of imbuing false concepts of freedom which will certainly render you a slave, not a genuinely free soul.

Five energy loves speed. It's quite common to see this mercurial number in the charts of people who engage in motion sports or activities. Dancing, skiing, swimming, martial arts, sports car, boat and horse racing, etc. are all within the domain of the Five's love of motion and movement. So is gambling because it offers a chance for fast money, as well as the excitement Fives enjoy, even crave. Speed is addictive, and if there is any number that rules speed, it is definitely the Five. Yet, speed kills. Its momentum can create situations beyond the control of its owner, resulting in dangerous to lethal consequences. Red flag here. Therefore, it's best to move at Divine Speed, that speed which allows you to remain in His Will, safe from harm.

Five is the Number of Man because all human beings have Five in common more than any other number: five fingers on each hand, five toes on each foot, five physical senses, thirty-two teeth; five rings on the Olympic flag. There are also 365 days in a year, a five in reduction. Too, Five is the fulcrum of the alpha-numeric spectrum, the pivot point of all the basic numbers. Therefore, it can move from one end to the other with equal ease. No number moves more easily than the Five. This ability not only gives it its facility of movement but an excellent ability to communicate with all people. And since it is the fulcrum of the Avenue of Crowns it must, more than any other number, exude balance in all things.

The main lesson for the Five is to learn the difference between freedom and slavery - the two sides of the Five energy coin. Freedom demands responsibility and self-control, and if these virtues are not respected and manifested, the result is slavery of all kinds - physical, emotional, financial, psychological, familial, spiritual. No one really wants to be a slave, and while Five is the apotheosis of freedom, it is also the greatest contender for becoming a slave . . . to itself.

Nature Energy: 6

With Six in the Nature or Material Nature your manner and way of doing things are centered in concepts of the heart, hearth, home, romance and community. You have a genuine warmth, gentleness and softness about you that is very attractive and comforting to people. You are the nurturer who gently smoothes the salve of love, compassion and concern on the wounds of people's lives. Potentially, you are an excellent mother, father, spouse, compassionate leader and loving personal friend. You are loyal and responsible and in most cases would rather stay at or near home and with the family than go gallivanting around the countryside devoid of any concern for those you love.

Six, of course, is two times Three, the cipher of self-expression and pleasure. Therefore, the negative side of the Six vibration can, like the Three, lead one down the path of excess, addiction, drug use, dangerous sexuality and hatred.

The positive aspect of the Six is that at its zenith, it is pure love, personal compassion, harmony, beauty and art. At its nadir, it is degenerate lust, hatred, envy, jealousy, bitterness, inharmony and ugliness - not of form but vibration. Six also has the indwelling condition of being the great nurturer or the great destroyer. Nothing hurts more than a wounded or broken heart. Contrarily, nothing is more radiant or joyful than a heart filled with pure love and compassion and, from a spiritual perspective, it is love, not passion, that creates joy, harmony and happiness and lifts the soul and psyche to wonderful levels of comfort, warmth and peace.

People with a Six Nature are most comfortable in domestic environments, especially if they're beautiful. Males often make excellent fathers, brothers, coaches, counselors, boy scout leaders and team players. Females under this energy generally love all things associated with family life from the kitchen to the baby's room and all points in between. They, too, make wonderful coachers, trainers, community leaders and organizers.

With a Six Nature, one caution is not to allow others to abuse your love and compassionate spirit. People may well take advantage if you're too giving, too concerned with their opinion of you. Also, be careful of becoming an enabler. There is such a thing as tough love, i.e., making people own up to their own actions, especially children. Being too soft at the wrong moment actually weakens and cripples children by teaching them there will always be someone to take care of them, which is not necessarily how real life works. Helping children learn to stand on their own two feet is critical to making them strong, responsible and mature adults who know the true meaning of love and compassion.

Nature Energy: 7

As a Seven Nature, your way and manner of doing things are centered in principles and concepts of thought, analysis, reflection, perfection, intuition, reclusion, research and privacy. You are a deep thinker and possibly introverted and shy. You consider your options and actions and reflect upon them as well. You also strive for perfection, seeking integration between the worlds of matter and spirit.

The Seven Nature is, potentially, the most spiritual vibration of its kind. Seven wends within. Therefore, you are pensive, quiet, separate, even distant from others. To them you may seem odd, cold and strange because you don't necessarily like to mix with others in the outer world of social activity. However, you are not necessarily cold or distant or strange - maybe to the outer world, but certainly not to the inner world. You are simply different, motivated by interests and desires unknown to those absorbed in the outer world of external phenomena, experiences and activity. Yes, you may like to be alone, but separation and isolation from the turmoil of day-to-day activity is important for you in order for you to access the inner regions of your mind and spirit. You need to have your private time and space to recharge your batteries.

Being alone, withdrawn, reclusive and liking your own company is natural to the Seven Nature. To discover deeper truths and live at a deep level mandates that you have to have time to and for yourself to ponder life and its critical questions. Living on the surface doesn't appeal to you unless you also maintain a good amount of Two, Four, Six or Eight energy in your Expression, Lifepath or PE. Seven is the most internal vibration in the Avenue of Crowns and it is not socially driven. It is internally driven. Since the world beats to an external, social drum, it is understandable that your solitary drumbeat resounds within, i.e., that internal and introverted place where you are most comfortable.

The Seven Nature not only makes you spiritually, religiously, metaphysically oriented, it also gives you a propensity to be poised, calm, quiet, reserved and elegant. Seven is very stately, august and noble. You hold your head well, and should, for yours is regal and worthy of a crown - not a crown of arrogance, but one of majestic humility, peace and grace.

The Seven Nature, because it likes its privacy and reclusiveness, is often seen as shy. Unfortunately, those living in the outer world mistake shyness for weakness rather than a manner of being. There is no law in the universe that says one has to be popular, gregarious or socially gifted to be whole or acceptable to God. In fact, it could well be argued that God Himself gave you a Seven Nature so you could move closer to Him, closer to the inner worlds of divine peace, bliss and love. So enjoy your sense of separation. Enjoy liking to be your own best friend and spending quality time alone. You need it and you deserve it.

A few cautions. First, because of its perfection-seeking, meticulous nature, the Seven can be too critical of others who don't share the same degree of precision as you. Therefore, being patient, soft and forgiving will go a long way to softening the appearance of a cold and calculating exterior. Second, be cautious of your tendency to be secretive. Privacy has its place, but when the Seven is too secretive, suspicions from loved ones may arise, creating concerns.

Third, just as the Seven can bring great light and wisdom, it can also bring great darkness and ignorance. Be very careful of walking on the dark side of life, of doing things in the ostensibly private shadows of untoward behaviors that your intuition may be telling you to avoid. Ostensible because nothing is hidden from God. As the Bible says, *Be sure your sins will find you out* [Numbers 32:23].

The Seven rules both saints and sinners . . . great saints and great sinners. The Light is pure and erases all shadows. The Dark is impure, adulterated and adulterates, hunting the precious life, destroying it and everything within its milieu. Darkness is ignorance and ignorance is no excuse before Divine Law when confronted with its actions, as it will be eventually. Many mystics, saints and godly people have the 88-16-7 energy in their charts, the most spiritual of all numbers. Yet, both Hitler and Stalin had the 88-16-7 energy in their charts too, a reflection of the dual nature of this world. Therefore, just as the 88-16-7 is the most spiritual of numbers, it is also the most evil, as is apparent in the lives of these nefarious and murderous men. It would be wise to heed this understanding.

Finally, as a Seven Nature individual, learn to love your sense of separation and isolation. Spiritual and mystic literature is replete with reassuring statements regarding the necessity of spending time alone. It is in your "alone time" that you have the opportunity to go within and make deep connections with the indwelling Spirit because, ultimately, the Path of Light is found Within, not without.

Nature Energy: 8

As an Eight Nature, your way and manner of doing things are concentrated in the areas of social interaction, success, commerce, business and external power. You are the one who likes to manage, lead, take charge. You definitely like to be in the center of all that flows. Generally speaking, you are quite social and enjoy mixing. Money, wealth, riches, material success, comfort, personal prestige, recognition and achievement are important to the Eight Nature because the Eight energy is the 'energy of the loop', of material success, leadership and management. Eight connects and disconnects. It sees what needs to be done and gets it done, usually by taking charge and managing others, administrating and coordinating all of the various tasks and duties essential to the efficient accomplishment and success of the project at hand.

The Lemniscate Eight Loop

Positive Pole [+]  [-] Negative Pole

Eight administrates. It also manipulates. Manipulation is not a bad word. Doctors and health care professionals, for example, manipulate people to better health as a course of their function. Generals, CEOs, presidents, executives and other leadership personnel are duty-bound to manipulate all of the components within the structural confines of their authority for the benefit of all who come within the boundaries of their jurisdiction. As an Eight Nature, you are a manipulator. You are the one who is responsible for connecting the opposing polar charges - positive and negative, buyer and seller, concept and completion, etc. The main concern, however, is that because you have these skills, you must use them for the good of all, not just the good of yourself. Selfish manipulation for personal gain creates untoward karmic payback. In other words, if you manipulate other people, situations or conditions negatively in this life, you will be manipulated in future lives. No mortal is powerful enough, bright enough or deceptive enough to manipulate karma law. So beware and take care. Use your skill wisely.

Eights have a natural propensity for being able to figure out how things work, how an idea, product, process, service, electrical current, etc. flows to create a continuous circuit. It's a wonderful trait. This is where the Eight shines - in knowing, or being able to figure out, how things work, whatever those things are. Because of this unique skill, people with Eight energy strongly dominate in their charts make excellent generals, admirals, administrators, presidents, CEOs, managers, mechanics, technicians, coaches, principals, doctors, police and fire captains, etc. - anything to do with solving problems through understanding "flow."

Because Eight is the highest octave of the social numbers Two, Four, Six and Eight, it is the most socially gifted and astute. Therefore, Eights are usually found in the socialite section of the local newspaper. Such people love to connect, interact, move and mix, be in the loop and in the center of all that's social.

As an Eight Nature, enjoy your social gifts. Be the organizer, leader, administrator, executive, mechanic. Be careful, however, that you remain patient with those people who are not as gifted as you are. Few people are. Knowing how to connect opposing polarities and make things function smoothly is a rare gift.

Nature Energy: 9

As a Nine Nature, you radiate a natural power and presence unmatched by the other basic numbers. Therefore, your way and manner of doing things are power-based and dominant. Your presence is always felt and is unmistakable. Because Nine is the grand elemental, its vibration encompasses all vibrations. You therefore have a propensity of attraction, an inherent magnetism that is real but untouchable and somewhat unexplainable.

Your Nine Nature gives you charisma and charm. There seems to be a completeness about you that the other basic natures lack. You are dynamic, and it is in your nature to rule, not be ruled. There is a strong possibility that, although you have a definite universal quality about you, you may tend to be more of a pubic figure and person than a private or personal one. Nine is not a personally loving vibration. It is a universally loving one. Your personality is rooted in the ability to connect with all people.

As a Nine Nature, you do not do things in a small way. Your energy is too expansive and all-inclusive for that. You encompass everything and there is a definite side to you that is dominant. Just be sure it does not become oppressively domineering. The Nine energy brings an enormous test of power, responsibility, humility, restraint and gracious generosity coupled with the refinement and bearing of a magnanimous monarch. Be this. Work to this level and avoid the pitfall of imperious, overbearing rulership which, karmically, will lead to indentured servitude of the worst sort.

Probably the greatest caution for the Nine Nature is in the use and misuse of power. The symbol for the Nine is the crown because Nines rule. Yet, rulership can be just as nefarious as it can be magnanimous. Power is power. It plays no favorites between the forces of light and darkness. In this regard, a quote from Shakespeare is germane: *Uneasy lies the head that wears a crown.* [Henry The Fourth, Part 2, Act 3, scene 1, 26–31]. And the Bard is not alone in his assessment of power. Here are some additional quotes for sentient thought.

> *Power tends to corrupt, and absolute power corrupts absolutely. Great men are almost always bad men.*
> ~ Lord Acton

> *No man is wise enough, nor good enough to be trusted with unlimited power.* ~ Charles Caleb Colton

Power, like a desolating pestilence, pollutes whatever it touches. ~ Percy Shelley

People with a Nine Nature would do very well in occupations and vocations set on the public stage such as doctors, nurses, dentists, lawyers, educators, actors, entertainers, writers, reporters, newscasters, authors, volunteers of all kinds, teachers, preachers, therapists, humanitarians - anything to do with the public stage and humanity in general. Nine is the energy belonging to everyone because it is everyone. When Nine Nature individuals understand this, they should be able to expand their own skills and abilities and elevate themselves into a limitless sky.

Chapter Seven

THE LOVELINE

The *Loveline* is the numeric blueprint of an individual's life through which the energies of love and attraction are realized. It is a simple template designating the seven Loveline [Basic Matrix] components we've discussed to this point: Lifepath, Expression, PE, Soul, Material Soul, Nature and Material Nature. We will use this Loveline to determine the secrets of our life, loves, and relationships. Following in Chapter Eight, *Love Match*, we will discover how to determine the love compatibility between us and another person. With a little study and practice, we can learn to do this in just 5 Minutes!

	The Loveline Components	
1	Lifepath	The *Script* of life
2	Expression	The person as *Actor* or *Actress*
3	Performance	The *Role* played
4	Soul	*Needs, Wants, Desires*-A
5	Material Soul	*Needs, Wants, Desires*-B
6	Nature	*Personality* and *Temperament*-A
7	Material Nature	*Personality* and *Temperament*-B

Component Review

Let's now review the seven components of the Loveline, i.e. Basic Matrix [*The King's Book of Numerology, Volume I: Foundations & Fundamentals*], which we've been studying to this point.

<u>A. Lifepath [PE]</u>: The script of one's life from the Birthdate.
1. Write down the birth date in this order: day- month-year. Spell the month in the first line for clarity [ex. 12 December 2009]
2. Convert the birthdate components to numbers [ex. 12-12-2009]
3. Add left to right and reduce to a single number.
   [ex. $1 + 2 + 1 + 2 + 2 + 0 + 0 + 9 > 17 > 1 + 7 = 8$]
   Lifepath is 8

<u>B. Expression [Exp]</u>: The actor/actress. The Full Birth name.
1. Write the name down on a piece of paper.
2. Place the number associated with each letter under it.
3. Add the numbers left to right and reduce to a single digit.

Simple Letter Value Chart									
The Letters	A	B	C	D	E	F	G	H	I
	J	K	L	M	N	O	P	Q	R
	S	T	U	V	W	X	Y	Z	
Number Value	1	2	3	4	5	6	7	8	9

C. Performance [PE]: The role the actor/actress plays in life.

    Formula: Lifepath + Expression = Performance

1. Add the Lifepath to the Expression; reduce to a single digit.

D. Soul: Desires, needs and wants [primary]

1. Write down the vowels: A-1 E-5 I-9 O-6 U-3 Y-7
2. Place the number associated with each vowel under it.
3. Add the numbers left to right and reduce to a single digit.

E. Material Soul [MS]: Desires, needs and wants [secondary]

    Formula: Soul + Lifepath = Material Soul

1. Add the Soul to the Lifepath and reduce to a single digit

F. Nature: Personality-Temperament [primary]

1. Write down the consonants.
2. Place the number associated with each consonant under it.
3. Add the numbers left to right and reduce to a single digit.

G. Material Nature [MN]: Personality-Temperament [secondary]

    Formula: Nature + Lifepath = Material Nature

1. Add the Nature to the Lifepath and reduce to a single digit.

Create the Loveline

    Let's now create the Lovelines for Mary Jane Smith and John David Doey.

1. Loveline of Mary Jane Smith: Born 8 January 1960

Mary Jane Smith: Born 8 January 1960	
Lifepath	7
Expression	3
Performance	1
Soul	5
Material Soul	3
Nature	7
Material Nature	5

2. Loveline of John David Doey: Born 14 August 1985

John David Doey Born 14 August 1985	
Lifepath	9
Expression	1
Performance	1
Soul	7
Material Soul	7
Nature	3
Material Nature	3

3. What's your Loveline?

Name: Born:	
Lifepath	
Expression	
Performance	
Soul	
Material Soul	
Nature	
Material Nature	

Reading the Loveline

Now that we've constructed the Loveline, how do we read it? The answer is that each number is represented by various *Keywords*. Reading the Loveline simply involves associating the numbers with their keywords. A *Keywords Catalogue* at the end of this chapter contains a working list of keywords. You will notice there are many keywords for each number. Basically, each keyword revolves around a central concept associated with its companion number, and many of the words are only synonyms. After working with the keywords, you'll become quite familiar with them and the concepts they represent.

Let's now expand Mary and John's Lovelines to include the keywords for each component. One of the cardinal points to remember in "reading" a Loveline is to remember what each of the Loveline components represents [see beginning of this chapter]. We'll just use a few words for example purposes. Eventually, as you become more skilled in this process, you'll be able to describe each of the Loveline components with a narrative description. Referring to the descriptions in each chapter will be helpful.

Mary Jane Smith: 8 January 1960 - Expanded Loveline

Expanded Loveline: Mary Jane Smith

Lifepath	7	Internal-Spirit-reflection-privacy-solitude
Expression	3	Image-Communication-words-joy-friends
Performance	1	Self-doer-leader-creator-pioneer-maverick
Soul	5	Freedom-adventure-motion-senses-fun
Material Soul	3	Image-Communication-words-joy-friends
Nature	7	Internal-Spirit-reflection-privacy-solitude
Material Nature	5	Freedom-adventure-motion-senses-fun

Narrative of Mary Jane Smith's Loveline

With a 7 Lifepath, Mary will have many experiences which will test her spiritual character. There will be times when she will be alone, if not physically, then mentally or emotionally. Events in her life will force her to examine her motives, actions, intentions. This 7 Lifepath portends a journey of reflection, research, analysis, internalization, separation, inquisition, asking why, probing life's most secret and sacred aspects. This is also the Lifepath that has the most potential for spiritual growth, but it will come at a price. Mary will endure many circumstances that test her spirit, potentially creating betrayals, confusion, sorrows, tears, even tragedies. Although this seems dire, it must be remembered that this is also the Lifepath that creates diamonds, deepens the spirit and transforms people into substantive souls of worth and merit.

Because Mary's Nature is also a 7, this gives her great ability to deal with the vicissitudes of her life. Mary is very mentally gifted, intuitive, private, a perfectionist and potentially reclusive. She does like and need her private time. She's a good student and teacher. Whatever her life throws at her, she will be able to manage it. She most likely is deeply connected to the Spirit within, and coupled with her life's experiences, she could likely become a gifted and wise teacher, counselor or mentor.

Mary's Expression and Material Soul are both 3s. This combined energy gives her a marvelous presence of joy and light and the energy to spread joy and light to other people. She maintains a very positive outlook on life, sees and finds the silver lining in every storm cloud, shares her optimism with everyone in her world; no doubt has many friends with whom she loves spending time; is extremely good with words and communication skills; has a solid self image and is most likely extremely attractive, perhaps even beautiful. She is a very approachable individual, easy to know and like. She no doubt carries a smile with her wherever she goes. Without question, Mary is a joy to be around. She may be a little moody and withdrawn from time to time because of her 7 Nature and a 7 Lifepath that will force her into times of separation, isolation, loneliness and reclusion, but overall she is a rather happy soul and very content with herself. When a Soul energy matches a person's Expression energy, in this case Mary's 3 Material Soul with her 3 Expression, the result is a person who is quite comfortable being in their own skin. Furthermore, Mary's 7 Nature matches her 7 Lifepath so she is quite comfortable with the path she's traveling. There is a good deal of harmony, therefore, between her desires, herself and her journey in life.

Besides having a dual 7 Lifepath and 7 Nature, as well as a dual 3 Expression and 3 Material Nature, Mary also maintains a third dual aspect in her chart - a 5 Soul and 5 Material Nature. This couplet gives Mary has an intense sense of her own freedom, diversity, adventure, movement, experience and sense enjoyment. With the fun-loving 3 energy, as well as the potentially wild carefree spirit of the 5, Mary will need to use discretion and self-control in her life. No two numbers together are more fun, exciting, pleasurable and sense-oriented than the 3 and 5. As long as these energies are controlled, they will create a life of joy, friends, pleasure, adventure, freedom, fun and memorable times. But if not controlled, they have the potential to wreak havoc in

Mary's life, especially given her 7 Lifepath which, given the combined intensity of the 3 and 5, will intensify her spiritual testing.

Mary's 1 Performance is going to make her extremely self-oriented, independent, a leader, a doer and self-starter, and coupled with her 7 Lifepath and 7 Nature, a loner from time to time. This may confuse the people in her life because she is outwardly a happy, joy-filled, adventurous, fun-loving, social individual. Yet, the 7 Lifepath will force her to evaluate her life because she will be spiritually tested. If she maintains a sense of self-control and ethical behavior, her later life will be positive and enjoyable. If she allows the 3 and 5 to run away with her, she may well have to face the tears of remorse, sorrow, sadness and regret.

With this particular set of energies, if Mary's parents had an understanding of numbers when she was a child, they could counsel her on the values of discipline, self-control, patience, centeredness and spiritual law. If lived to the highest level of each number, Mary will have an extraordinary life of friends, fun, adventure, independence and good times. The rub to this scenario, however, is the 7 Lifepath. It's very telling. There is no doubt Mary will be tested spiritually, ethically, morally. If she passes the tests as they arrive, and there will be many tests, she will move up the ladder of the spirit. If she fails the tests, or fails more than she passes, her life could give her more grief than she would like. Whether she plants beneficial seeds or deleterious seeds is her choice, of course. However, it would be extremely wise for her to remember that sometimes life doesn't give second chances and to act accordingly.

John David Doey: 14 August 1985 - Expanded Loveline

Expanded Loveline: John David Doey

Lifepath	9	Public stage; art; humanity; recognition
Expression	1	Self-doer-leader-creator-pioneer-maverick
Performance	1	Self-doer-leader-creator-pioneer-maverick
Soul	7	Internal-Spirit-reflection-privacy-solitude
Material Soul	7	Internal-Spirit-reflection-privacy-solitude
Nature	3	Image-Communication-words-joy-friends
Material Nature	3	Image-Communication-words-joy-friends

Narrative of John David Doey's Loveline

John's 9 Lifepath is going to take him on a journey through the public domain in some capacity. He may well travel abroad, as 9 rules travel, but it is a sure thing that his 9 life's script will place him among the masses, in contact with many people. The 9 Lifepath is the most expansive and universal of all the lifepaths.

There is a chance John could well be an educator, doctor, lawyer, writer, producer, director, newscaster, reporter, minister, counselor, medical examiner, actor. This is because of the large amount of 1, 3 and 7 energy to compliment the 9. John's double 1s in his Expression and Performance make him very independent, self-actuating, self-reliant. He is a doer and a creator, definitely his own person. The 1 energy can be very strong-willed and John has it in two of the strongest components of his loveline. He himself is the independent creator, doer and leader and the role of his life is the same. Furthermore, John's 1 Expression passes through the funnel of his 9 Lifepath [or mixes with it] to create his 1 PE. By passing through the 9 LP, the 1 gathers strength, power and a public persona, creating an even more intense 1 PE. No two numbers are more personally dominant than the 1 and 9 in combination. The 1 leads; the 9 rules. Therefore, John's life is going to be very centered in himself working with the public.

Because John's Soul and Material Soul are both 7s, the desires motivating him are internal. He's not concerned with the business world per se [8 energy], or working as a clerk or holding a service-oriented job [4 energy]. He desires to use his mind and thought. He loves to research, examine, reflect, think, study, teach and spend time alone. John is definitely not a social butterfly. His double dose of 1 energy in his Expression and PE, as well as his double dose of 7 in his Soul and Material Soul make him very solitary and separate. No two numbers acting in concert are more separated from the social masses more than the 1 and 7. Whatever John does with his life, he will be spending time alone, even if it's in his head. Chances are very good, however, that he will seek the solace, comfort and privacy of a self-created sanctuary such as a personal office, private residence, cabin in the woods, etc. Even though he may prefer a retreat in the mountains, it's unlikely that with a 9 Lifepath he'll get it unless he becomes a park ranger.

John's double 3s in his Nature and Material Nature give him an extremely approachable persona. He's very positive; good with words; loves to communicate; spend time with friends, and enjoy life. There's an excellent possibility that because of all his 1, 3 and 7 energy, John could be a writer, actor or educator, especially given his 9 Lifepath. The 3 and 7 together are a writer's combination with the mind and its thought [7] giving expression through words and communication [3]. This 3-7 combo can also be expressed through religion, metaphysics and spirituality. As we've read, 7 is the most sacred of all the basic numbers. It's the most mentioned number in the Bible. The number 3 also has sacred dimensions as it is the number for the Trinity.

In a nutshell, John is a very independent, self-actuating individual [1] with deep desires to know, question, examine, reflect, analyze and study [7] while he exudes an excellent ability with words and communication [3] as he traverses an expansive lifepath filled with people and the public stage [9].

The double 3 energy in John's Soul and Material Soul also address health and well-being. Coupled with his keen desire for knowledge, there is a good chance he will be focused on health both for himself and others. Remember, his 9 Lifepath governs the public stage and his 3 Soul has to funnel, filter or mix with the 9 before it becomes transformed into his 3 Material Soul, making his 3 Material Soul more publically expansive than his regular Soul energies. As a note, the only people who will have identical Soul and Material Soul ciphers like John will be people who also possess a 9 Lifepath. The same goes for the Nature and Material Nature. Thus, the 9 energy magnifies the power in a chart in more ways than one.

What is interesting about both John and Mary's charts is that both of them contain only odd numbers. Notice there are no social numbers in their Lovelines; no 2-4-6-8. Therefore, neither is highly social, although both are pleasant, artistic, creative. John's life is more public because of his 9 Lifepath. Mary's life is more adventurous because of her double 5 energy in her Soul and Material Nature. Age difference aside, John and Mary are very compatible as we'll see in Chapter Eight, *Love Match*.

Keywords

Keywords define and describe numbers. After we've established the Loveline and its seven numeric components, the next step is to associate each number with its *keywords* and phrases. Following is a *Keywords Catalogue* of the nine basic numbers for our reference purposes. An excellent learning tool is to establish our own chart and, using the *keywords*, create a description of each of the Loveline components as they apply to us. No one knows us like we know ourselves. Following is a blank extended Loveline. As an exercise, fill in your data, use the *keywords catalogue* to list a few words germane to your life and then write a brief narrative of your own life like that of Mary and John. It's a fun way to learn the entire process. The next step would be to create a Loveline for people you know well. Doing this is arguably the best way to learn. Once you've acquired some skills, and it won't take long, you'll be able to create a Loveline in just 5 minutes and have a fairly clear picture of the person whether you know them personally or not.

Extended Loveline for:_____

	#	Brief List of Keywords
Lifepath		
Expression		
Performance		
Soul		
Material Soul		
Nature		
Material Nature		

Narrative: Get some paper, a pen or a keyboard and start writing!

Keywords Catalogue

Note 1: Every number maintains a positive and negative aspect (polarity), just as every coin has two sides. Furthermore, we cannot hold a coin without holding both sides simultaneously. The same is true for numbers, and our lives reflect both the positive and negative aspects of each vibration to some degree. In other words, no number is perfect, no chart is perfect, no human being is perfect. We all have assets and liabilities, good qualities and bad qualities, and we all walk with the light and dark simultaneously.

Note 2: It would be impossible to list every word in the English language which is attached to each of the nine basic numbers. After all, there are only nine basic numbers and hundreds of thousands of words. Therefore, a complete keyword list would be impossible to generate.

ONE - 1

Primal Force, first cause, genesis, yang, fire, ego, self, man, male, individual, individuality, independent, independence, masculine, father, identity, leader, director, doer, creator, creativity, authority figure, boss, activator, initiator, pioneer, star, center of attention, maverick, lone wolf, solo, direct, unique, original, skill, will, raw power, self-confidence, vitality, action, self-control, self-sufficiency, determination, activates, initiates, creates, creation, dominates, leads, attains, driving, strong, courageous, powerful, dynamic, decisive, unbending, steadfast, dominant, linear, single-minded, starts, new beginnings, assertive, aggressive, overbearing, self-indulgent, ego-maniacal, selfish, self-obsessed, tom-boy, rational, reasonable, logical, unemotional, radiating, initiating, purpose, direction.

TWO - 2

Yin, water, woman, female, feminine, mother, daughter, sister, others, relationships, helper, assistant, support, supporter, separate, separation, division, adversity, adversary, adversarial, assistance, cooperative, cooperation, collaboration, contention, confliction, consideration, competition, opposition, vacillation, follower, dependent, diplomatic, duality, duplicity, deceit, teamwork, partnership, passive, patient, non-obtrusive, intuitive, receptive, responsive, agreeable, amenable, affable, kind, warm, devoted, sweet, gentle-hearted, peacemaking, harmonizing, equalizing, submissive, rhythm, rhythmic, equalizing, equilibrium, indecisive, rivalry, intuitive, behind the scenes, bending, yielding, non-assertive, together, taking sides, irrational, illogical, unreasonable, emotion, emotional, reflecting (as in the Moon reflecting light, water reflecting an image), absorbing (vs. radiating of the 1), acquiescing, us vs. them, war and peace.

THREE - 3

Trinity, triads, air sign, the triangle (Ancient symbol of Perfection), The Golden Mean of Aristotle, Yin and Yang in perfect balance (the symbol of the Tao), art, artistry, artistic, words, communication, self-expression, personal integration, fulfillment, health, beauty, vanity, happiness, wholeness, holiness, holistic, well-being, vibrant, alive, creative, sex, marriage, children, joy, enjoyment, pleasure, parties, friends, good times, talkative, verbal, gregarious, approachable, gossip, social, outgoing, fun-loving, entertaining, entitled, entitlement, spoiled, lighthearted, imaginative, happy, optimistic, cheerful, charming, embracing, writing, acting, performing, glamorous, ease, disease, dis-ease, hostility, poisonous words, harsh, critical, criticism, stern, vain, egotistical, narcissistic.

FOUR - 4

Earth, order, structure, work, service, security, stability, framework, form, foundation, boundaries, rules, regulations, guidelines, routine, status quo, commitment, construction, limitation, restriction, constriction, concrete, duty, discipline, dependability, effort, control, confines, proprieties, mechanics, servant, matter, materialism, transformation, transmutation, confined, confinement, toil, physical strength, solid power, steadfast, sturdy, the rock, anchor, roots, chains, obstacles, tradition, convention, loyalty, prudent, clerical, industrious, down to earth, frugal, practical, organizing and organization, house, beams, foundations, constancy, regimentation, classification, systemize, non-adventurous, predictable, obstinate, resistant, recalcitrant, boring, patterns, plodding along, negative aspects are: insecure, unstable, unfaithful, dishonest, weak, insecure.

FIVE - 5

The Number of Man, the fulcrum of the alpha-numeric spectrum, free, freedom, fire, change, loss, motion, movement, detachment, detaching, diverse, diversity, versatility, shifting, speed, wild, careless, adventure, adventurous, roam, roaming, liberation, liberate, unrestrained, undisciplined, non-restriction, nonrestrictive, shifts, slavery, mercurial, spontaneous, exciting, excitement, experience, experiential, variety, talent, people, senses, sexuality, sensations, stimulation, energy, mercurial, multi-faceted, many sided, assortment, exuberant, enthusiastic, foot-loose, flamboyant, dashing, energetic, exploring, exposure, exhibitionist, travel, unpredictable, unconventional, uncertain, unstable, instability, the crowd, letting go, free-spirited, rebellious, liberation, liberating, stimulating, stimulants, non-complacent, temptation, temperance, restraint, indulgence, animated, exuberant, volatile.

SIX - 6

Love and hate, home, hearth, matters of the heart, romance, domesticity, domicile, water, emotion, adjustability, responsibility, accountability, personal love, art, artistic, beauty, community, harmonious, harmonizing, caring, warm, nurturing, understanding, soft, comfortable, dependable, conscientious, kind, responsive, music, sex, singing, hatred, cruelty, family discord, family issues and concerns, addiction, jealousy, envy, resentment, bitterness, acrimony.

SEVEN - 7

Spirit, spiritual, mystical, sacred, air sign, internal, internalization, bliss, peace, quiet, calm, centeredness, noble, nobility, ignobility, ignominy, chaos, chaotic, analysis, thought, the thinker, intuition, introspection, investigation, inquisition, reflection, research, examination, contemplation, recession, receding, repose, reclusive, reclusion, distancing, counseling, alienation, study, student, teacher, testing, reflecting, evaluating, reviewing, learning, processing, separate, isolation, separation, seclusion, secrecy, secret, stealthy, privacy, private, religion, rest, quiet, tranquility, inwardness, the 'within', perfection, poise, wisdom, curious, distant, deep, cool, cold, removed, withdrawn, recede, shy, reserved, refined, non-social, purify, purification, alone, isolated, alienated, stressed, distressed, troubled, turmoil, tumult, tribulation, unworldly, thoughtful or thoughtless, investigative, trouble, problems, worry, concern, scandal, scandalous, misery, miserable.

EIGHT - 8

Earth sign, external power, flow, social importance, interaction, involvement, connection, disconnection, orchestration, integration, coordination, circulation, manipulation, administration, execution, association, continuation, continuity, opportunity, opportunistic, opportunist, responsive and non-responsive, mixing, karmic conduit, circuits, circulate, systems, worldly success-power-wealth, materialism, material comfort, management, marketing, promotion, commerce, business, efficiency of motion-movement-management, being in the loop, administrator, commander, executive, generalship, governorship, coordinating, socialization, socializing, leadership, organization, usury, externalization, the 'without'.

NINE - 9

The Grand Elemental, the Number of Mankind, rulership, universality, timeless, charismatic, magnetic, macrocosm, the universal giver, the world, worldly, the public stage and spotlight, the 'many,' humanitarian, humanitarianism, impersonal love, healer, healing, travel, the universal languages of music, art, acting, the theater, theatrical, thespian, endings, conclusions, completions, climaxes, terminations, the Chameleon, volunteer, inclusions, broadcast, broadcaster, broadcasting, public exposure, expansion, magnanimous, regal, royal, philanthropic, philosophical, education, educator, all encompassing, understanding, generous, tolerant, broad-minded, global, strong, dominant, domineering, controlling, intensity of emotion, strong, overbearing, imperious, arrogant.

Chapter Eight

LOVE MATCH

Numbers rule the universe. Everything is arranged according to number and mathematical shape.

Pythagoras

Just as "numbers rule the universe," they rule everything in the universe including love and attraction between people. It may seem unbelievable, even fantastic, but it is true. By correlating the Loveline numbers of two people, we can know if there is enough attraction between them to generate a meaningful relationship. Whether the relationship lasts depends on other factors in each of the individual's destinies, but when the numbers are arranged in the appropriate locations, there will be attraction. Furthermore, this can be generally accomplished in a matter of a few minutes.

How can this be? What we have to remember is that each of us is actually energy, not merely flesh, muscles, blood and bone. Numbers are merely labels describing the energy fields comprising each of us. When the energies of our Loveline harmonize with those in another person's Loveline, there's attraction, which is really the basis of love in a worldly sense.

The Love Match Process

The Love Matching process consists of three components: 1. *Loveline Matrix*; 2. *Loveline Mix*; 3. *Loveline Keys*. The process consists of following three easy steps:

1. Create a *Loveline Matrix*

    The Loveline Matrix is a juxtaposition of the Lovelines of the people involved so the numbers [energies] can be easily read. Each Loveline includes the seven basic components we've studied thus far plus the first names of each person. After this is constructed, give it a read.

    Note: in the Loveline Matrix the top three components, the Lifepath, Expression and Performance [PE] are referred to as the *Umbrella* or *External* part of the person's life. The lower five components are referred to as the *Internal* or *Hidden* aspects of the individual. Note: in an excellent love match, both the External and Internal aspects of each person's chart will be fulfilled.

2. Create a *Loveline Mix*

    The Loveline Mix is a simple form that creates a third element, the *Mix,* which is the addition of the separate components of each person, thus creating a centralized third column or entity, the relationship itself. In the love process, some people may be attracted to the other person or to the mix of energies between them or both. The *Mix* is a real living energy/entity and through it we can see if the relationship is going to be smooth, bumpy or conflictive.

3. Apply the *Loveline Keys*

The *Loveline Keys* are the fundamental connections that create attraction and love between people. Note: identical numbers in identical components of the Lovelines do not necessarily create a romantic love connection because if identical numbers reside in the same components of each person's chart, then each person is basically a clone of himself and this may not serve to fulfill the basic needs of each individual which must be satisfied if both the individuals are going to find love and fulfillment in the relationship. Therefore, it's critical to focus on the *Loveline Keys* because they are, indeed, the keys to love and attraction.

Loveline Matrix: Mary & John

To begin understanding this process, let's establish a Loveline Matrix between our two fictitious friends, Mary Jane Smith and John David Doey. Even though Mary is twenty-five years older than John [she was born in 1960; he in 1985], this will not affect their basic relationship, which is built on energy. Energies are energies. They are what create relationships [good or bad], not social conventions, nor age, regardless of the type of relationship that exists, such as a familial connection of parent to child, a romance between lovers, a bond between friends or a business alliance. In fact, a person born today may be extremely attracted to an historic figure of the distant past because their numbers mix and match wonderfully. Remember, it's primal energy that attracts or repels individuals one to the other regardless of time, race, creed, color or other external factors. Numbers, as energy, rule not just the universe but human relationships as well.

Loveline Matrix
Mary & John

		Mary	John		
External	Lifepath	7	9	Lifepath	External
	Expression	3	1	Expression	
	P/E	1	1	P/E	
Internal	Soul	5	7	Soul	Internal
	Material Soul	3	7	Material Soul	
	Nature	7	3	Nature	
	Material Nature	5	3	Material Nature	
	First Name	3	2	First Name	

In looking over the *Loveline Matrix* between Mary and John, we note the eight components of each as a double line separating the umbrella [external three components at the top of the grid] from the internal components below the double line. Since we've now established their Loveline Matrix, it's now time to study the *Loveline Keys* to determine what to look for in a relationship matrix.

Loveline Matrix Keys

1. Soul Release

Soul Release is <u>the most important factor</u> in determining whether a person will be fulfilled in a relationship because it satisfies the *internal* desires of a person, i.e., their most basic needs, wants and desires. If there is no *soul release*, the possibilities of an individual being content and happy with the relationship are greatly diminished. Optimally, if both parties have *soul release* the prospects of a very loving relationship are wonderfully enhanced.

S*oul Release* is when either one of an individual's soul components [the Natural Soul or Material Soul] match one of the three umbrella components - Lifepath, Expression or PE, preferably the Expression or Performance, of the other person. As we know, the Soul identifies the needs, wants, desires and motivations of a person. It is the core of the individual, the very center of who they are. When a person has his needs, wants and desires met, he or she is fulfilled. If those most basic and primal needs are not met, no matter how decent, good, pure, kind, noble, successful or universally loved the other person is, there will not be optimum attraction nor personal fulfillment.

Why the match between the Soul and the Umbrella? The Umbrella represents the outer aspect of a person's life. When the most internal and hidden aspect of the individual, the Soul, matches the most external aspect of the other person, there is a *release* of that person's energies to the outside world. They feel free, not trapped or frustrated. If there is no match, and hence no release for the individual's most primal and basic needs, wants and desires, there is a feeling of being trapped, suffocated, frustrated, unhappy, discontented. There are factors in the Loveline Matrix that may mitigate the frustration, but as a major rule, if there is no Soul release there will definitely be some degree of angst and unhappiness.

Why are the Expression and Performance components of the other person's Umbrella preferable to the Lifepath? Because the Expression is who the person is. The Performance is the role the person is playing on the great life stage. But the Lifepath has no personal energy. It is merely the script of a person's life. Therefore, if one person's Soul energies find release through the other person [his partner's Expression], or PE [the person's life role - a mixture of the Expression and Lifepath], the connection between them becomes harmonious, the Expression being the most personal and therefore the best match. The Lifepath can give satisfaction to a degree, but not on a personal level. These three combinations of the Soul [Natural or Material] would be:

Soul Release

1. Soul to Expression
2. Soul to Performance-Experience [PE]
3. Soul to Lifepath

For a person to be fulfilled, only one of their Soul components needs to find an umbrella match through the other person. If both Soul components find a match, all the better, but at least one of the two must find some degree of *release*.

Is it critical that both partners have *soul release*? This double soul release one to the other is optimum for a great relationship, but good relationships can and do exist when only one partner is satisfied. This is because when one person is satisfied, that person tends to make the other person happy.

Although *soul release* is best connected to the umbrella of the other person, the Soul energies can find release through their partner's Nature [Natural Nature or Material Nature] because the Nature represents the personality. It's not as strong a connection as the Umbrella but it works. A Soul to Nature connection can, therefore, create a degree of *soul release*.

Is there any *soul release* between Mary and John? Let's take a look.

Loveline Matrix
Mary's Soul Release

		Mary	John		
External	Lifepath	7	9	Lifepath	External
	Expression	3	1	Expression	
	P/E	1	1	P/E	
Internal	Soul	5	7	Soul	Internal
	Material Soul	3	7	Material Soul	
	Nature	7	3	**Nature**	
	Material Nature	5	3	**Material Nature**	
	First Name	3	2	First Name	

Here we see that Mary has a Material *soul release* through John's Nature and Material Nature. This is a definite plus for the relationship. Mary has a deep desire for joy, self-expression, words, communication, pleasure, art, good times, friendliness and ease of living. Both John's Nature and Material Nature match Mary's needs. However, her most primal desires represented by the 5 of freedom, variety, change, movement and exploration are not satisfied through John. This is not severely problematic because part of her needs are fulfilled and the 3 and 5 are both odd numbers, so they fall into the same polarity field, which is an harmonious connection. It is also a plus that Mary's First Name with its 3 cipher matches John's Nature and Material Nature.

An interesting aspect of Mary's Loveline is that her Material Soul and First Name match her Expression. This is a positive correspondence for Mary whether she is in a relationship or not. Individuals whose Soul energy matches a component in their umbrella, especially the Expression or PE, are generally very comfortable with themselves because they are [Expression] what they desire to be [Soul energy]. If their PE matches their Soul, then the performance they would be giving in life would also resonate with their basic desires, needs and wants, fulfilling them. If the Lifepath matches their Soul, then their desires are being fulfilled through their life's script. This is one reason why some people are very collected, calm and complete. There's an intrinsic harmonic connection between the internal and external aspects of their lives.

Let's now look at John's Loveline and its potential for *soul release*.

Loveline Matrix
John's Soul Release

		Mary	John		
External	**Lifepath**	7	9	Lifepath	External
	Expression	3	1	Expression	
	P/E	1	1	P/E	
Internal	Soul	5	7	**Soul**	Internal
	Material Soul	3	7	**Material Soul**	
	Nature	7	3	Nature	
	Material Nature	5	3	Material Nature	
	First Name	3	2	First Name	

Here we see that John is very connected to Mary, more so than she is to him. Both of his Soul energies connect to Mary's Lifepath and Nature, creating a *quadline*, a four point connection [two for his Soul and two for his Material Soul]. This is extremely favorable for their relationship. John loves his seclusion and privacy, as well as his analytical, quiet and inward-dwelling spirit. Mary's Nature matches these qualities. Too, her 7 Lifepath will bring to her the type of things that John loves even though his own Lifepath does not. This is where people's lives can be extremely enhanced - by having their most primal needs, wants and desires satisfied through another person's loveline when such desires are not satisfied through their own personal loveline.

An assessment can now be made that both Mary's and John's most basic needs are satisfied one through the other. This bodes extremely well for a good relationship on the merit of this aspect of their *Loveline Match* alone.

2. Expression to Performance [E-PE Link]

Expression to Performance [Expression to PE, the *E-PE Link*], is the second most important factor in determining the attraction and love in a relationship. As *soul release* governs the *internal* aspect of the relationship, the *E-PE Link* rules the *external* aspect. As everything in this creation has two sides, so do our relationships. The umbrella and its *E-PE Link* satisfies the outer part of relationship life - the activities, careers and roles played.

When one person's Expression equals the other person's Performance, there is resonance in the external lives of both individuals because one person [Expression] is in reality what the other person is acting out [Performance]. Thus, they may well like doing and sharing the same things, moving in the same direction, harmonizing on major external levels. They'll be good friends, buddies, companions, partners, teammates. Their lives won't cause a great deal of friction or problems between them. It will be pretty much smooth sailing. With both the *Soul Release* and *E-PE Line* harmonizing, both the internal and external aspects of the relationship find comfort, ease, joy and happiness. It is not necessary that both individuals have an *E-PE Line*. Only one is necessary for a good relationship; two are preferred for a great one.

Although the *E-PE Line* is the best external connection, an Expression to Expression or Expression to Lifepath are also good connections. The main thing is that there must be some form of external connection in the umbrella of the partners to insure a resonance of life's general activities.

The problem, however, arises when there is no outer connection. Even if there is *soul release*, if there is nothing on the outside of the life paradigm, there won't be a complete connection between the people involved, especially partners and spouses. To reiterate, for a relationship to be completely fulfilling, the optimum condition is that both the internal and external aspects of each person must be satisfied for a fruitful, happy, harmonious and loving relationship to exist in its most resplendent state.

Let's now check out Mary's and John's Loveline connections to see if this external connection exists in their umbrella.

Loveline Matrix: External [Umbrella] Connections
Mary & John

		Mary	John		
External	Lifepath	7	9	Lifepath	External
	Expression	3	1	Expression	
	P/E	1	1	P/E	
Internal	Soul	5	7	Soul	Internal
	Material Soul	3	7	Material Soul	
	Nature	7	3	Nature	
	Material Nature	5	3	Material Nature	
	First Name	3	2	First Name	

Bingo! Mary and John have an *E-PE Link*, his 1 Expression to her 1 Performance. This is positively compounded with their mutual 1 PEs. Thus, both are quite independent, self-reliant, and action-oriented. They each have an intrinsic understanding of the other's life and its activities. Coupled with their mutual *soul release*, the relationship between Mary and John is very good. They will enjoy being with each other and doing the same things.

If there were an umbrella connection but no *soul release*, only one aspect of their mutual relationship lives would be fulfilled, the external one. This doesn't mean their relationship would not be good, but it wouldn't be as complete and fulfilling as it would be if both internal and external aspects of their Lovelines were satisfied. Thus, when assessing two people for a successful and potentially life-long relationship such as marriage, it is recommended that both partners share an internal and external connection between them. This is the basis for a most loving and meaningful relationship.

3. Nature Release

Although not as powerful as the *Soul Release* or *Expression to PE*, the *Nature Release* plays an important role as well in the *Love Bond*. Located in the *internal* hemisphere, if the Nature or Material Nature connects to any of the Umbrella components of the other person there will be resonance and subsequent release. The difference between the *Soul Release* and the *Nature Release* is that the Soul defines the individual's deepest desires, needs and wants; the Nature defines the personality. Desires trump personality. It is our desires that motivate us and bring us contentment when they are fulfilled, so their release has greater potential for generating personal satisfaction. Yet, the *Nature Release* does have merit because its release creates a resonance of the personality with the energies of another individual.

The Nature of one person matching the Nature of another person creates resonance and familiarity but not necessarily release. The problem, as discussed earlier, is that when one

Loveline component matches the same component in the Loveline of another person, for example a 8 Nature of one person matching an 8 Nature of another person, a cloning effect is generated which doesn't necessarily serve to fulfill the individual. It may help him understand the other person but not offer any release of his own energies. After all, who wants to be loved by themselves? Even the most extreme narcissist would be challenged because in loving oneself there is no external attraction to warm the individual from without. It's a pretty safe bet to assume that most of us prefer to be loved, recognized, cherished and nurtured by someone else, not ourselves.

Let's check the Lovelines of Mary and John to see if they share any *Nature Release*.

Loveline Matrix
Mary's Nature Release

		Mary	**John**		
External	Lifepath	7	9	Lifepath	External
	Expression	3	1	Expression	
	P/E	1	1	P/E	
Internal	Soul	5	7	**Soul**	Internal
	Material Soul	3	7	**Material Soul**	
	Nature	7	3	Nature	
	Material Nature	5	3	Material Nature	
	First Name	3	2	First Name	

Indeed, Mary does have a Nature connection with John's Soul and Material Soul. This adds more power to their relationship. It works in reverse, of course, as a *Soul Release* for John.

Too, Mary's Nature also matches her own Lifepath. As her 3 Material Soul and 3 First Name match her 3 Expression, this 7

Nature matching her 7 Lifepath corroborates personal wholeness, thus strengthening her sense of self.

Loveline Matrix
John's Nature Release

		Mary	John		
External	Lifepath	7	9	Lifepath	External
	Expression	3	1	Expression	
	P/E	1	1	P/E	
Internal	Soul	5	7	Soul	Internal
	Material Soul	3	7	Material Soul	
	Nature	7	**3**	**Nature**	
	Material Nature	5	**3**	**Material Nature**	
	First Name	3	2	First Name	

John's 3 Nature and 3 Material Nature find enormous release through Mary's Loveline, specifically in her Expression, Material Soul and First Name, "Mary." This gives him six connections to Mary. Again, this adds to the overall positive connectivity between the two individuals.

4. Total Loveline Connections

A fourth key to determining the *Love Bond* is simply to calculate the total number of connections between the Lovelines of the individuals involved. These Loveline connections are the energetic glue and adhesive that keep the relationship together. The more glue, the more connections, the stronger the bond. Therefore, should the winds of life confront the relationship, it is more capable of weathering the storm and continuing its journey in tact. To determine these connections, we simply take each component of one Loveline and match it to other ciphers existing in the other person's Loveline. Connections are in parenthesis.

Loveline Matrix
Mary's Total Connections

		Mary	John		
External	Lifepath	7 [2]	9	Lifepath	External
	Expression	3 [2]	1	Expression	
	P/E	1 [2]	1	P/E	
Internal	Soul	5 [0]	7	Soul	Internal
	Material Soul	3 [2]	7	Material Soul	
	Nature	7 [2]	3	Nature	
	Material Nature	5 [0]	3	Material Nature	
	First Name	3 [2]	2	First Name	
Mary's Connections: 12					

Loveline Matrix
John's Total Connections

		Mary	John		
External	Lifepath	7	9 [0]	Lifepath	External
	Expression	3	1 [1]	Expression	
	P/E	1	1 [1]	P/E	
Internal	Soul	5	7 [2]	Soul	Internal
	Material Soul	3	7 [2]	Material Soul	
	Nature	7	3 [3]	Nature	
	Material Nature	5	3 [3]	Material Nature	
	First Name	3	2 [0]	First Name	
John's Connections: 12					

Through this combining process, we see that both Mary and John each have 12 Loveline connections to the other person. With a total of 24 combined connections, this bodes very well for the relationship between Mary and John, i.e., it's a lot of good glue.

5. Loveline Polarity

One of the keys to the Love Match is assessing the general polarity of the Loveline numbers. In Mary's and John's charts, we see that all the numerical components are odd numbers except for the first name of "John" which is a 2. This is very rare. Usually charts are a blend of both odd and even numbers. Still, in this particular case, with each of the individuals having a plethora of odd numbers, the relationship between them would be strong.

All in all, the Love Match between Mary and John is exceptionally positive. They both have *Soul Release* [the most important ingredient of relationship fulfillment]; *Expression to PE* [the second most critical element overall and the most important external connection]; each also has *Nature Release*; a combination of 24 connections between their Loveline and practically all odd numbers. Seeing this, we can conclude that the relationship between Mary Jane Smith and John David Doey is a good one and should bring attraction, love and fulfillment to each.

Following are two blank Loveline Matrices. What's your Love Match to that special individual in your life? Is there *Soul Release*? *Expression to PE*? *Nature Release*? How many total connections between the Lovelines? Is there a preponderance of one polarity over the other?

Loveline Matrix

_____ & _____

	Person # 1			Person # 2	
External	Lifepath			Lifepath	**External**
	Expression			Expression	
	P/E			P/E	
Internal	Soul			Soul	**Internal**
	Material Soul			Material Soul	
	Nature			Nature	
	Material Nature			Material Nature	
	First Name			First Name	
	Total Connections: Person #1 =				
	Total Connections: Person #2 =				

Loveline Matrix

_____ & _____

	Person # 1			Person # 2	
External	Lifepath			Lifepath	**External**
	Expression			Expression	
	P/E			P/E	
Internal	Soul			Soul	**Internal**
	Material Soul			Material Soul	
	Nature			Nature	
	Material Nature			Material Nature	
	First Name			First Name	
	Total Connections: Person #1 =				
	Total Connections: Person #2 =				

As we've seen, The Love Matrix is a great tool for relationship assessment and analysis. Yet, there's more . . . the *Love Mix*.

Notes:

Your Love Numbers   King

Chapter Nine

LOVE MIX

Through the Love Match we are able to focus on how our personal energies resonate with those of another person. Through the *Love Mix* we are able to see the relationship itself and how each individual relates to it.

People are energy. Relationships are energy. In fact, just as people are living entities of divine energy, so the relationship is a living entity of divine energy too. As each person has a life of his own, so each relationship has a life of its own . . . and it is real.

In a mundane scientific sense, each of us is a composite of basic elements and their molecules, atoms and subatomic particles. These combine into flesh, muscle, blood, bone and brain to form a human being. Yet, at our core, we are energy. Certainly, our spirits are pure energy. When we see ourselves as fields of living energy as opposed to material forms in the shape of bodies, our perspective changes. Material bodies don't mix. They can come together and touch but they don't really merge one into the other. But energy fields can mix in ways bodies cannot. By seeing ourselves, therefore, as energy rather than simple bags of blood and bone, we begin to perceive life and relationship on a whole new level, the level of interacting energy fields.

The encouragement, then, is for us to move beyond seeing ourselves as just physical bodies to seeing ourselves as energy spheres. When we see ourselves and others in this manner - as energy entities, we move to a depth of understanding that transcends the boundaries of matter and its inherent limitations.

The *Love Mix* is based in this idea of energetic perception of one person, as energy, literally mixing with another person, also as energy, to create a third energetic entity, the relationship. Therefore, when we come together in relationship with another person, the energy field that is us mixes with the energy field that is the other person to produce a very real third energy field, the relationship, and all of these living entities can be identified with numbers, which are nothing more than identifying labels for the energy fields themselves.

The Love Mix Process

The process of generating the *Love Mix* [aka, Loveline Mix] is extremely quick and easy, though highly effective. Using an expanded template of the Loveline Matrix, we will simply add the components of each individual, reduce them to a single digit and then associate them with the keywords to discern the characteristics of the relationship.

Following is the Loveline Mix of Mary and John. We'll first compute the total number of connections for each of them as we did with the Loveline Match, and then give a brief synopsis of how their Love Mix affects each of them. The Mix connection totals for each partner will be a composite of the ciphers of Loveline Match and the Mix.

Loveline Mix: Connections
Mary and John

	Mary	#1	Mix	#2	John	
External	Lifepath	7	**7**	9	Lifepath	External
	Expression	3	**4**	1	Expression	
	P/E	1	**2**	1	P/E	
Internal	Soul	5	**3**	7	Soul	Internal
	Material Soul	3	**1**	7	Material Soul	
	Nature	7	**1**	3	Nature	
	Material Nature	5	**8**	3	Material Nature	
	First Name	3	**5**	2	First Name	

Total Connections: Mary = 21
Total Connections: John = 21
Total Connections for Mary & John = 42

This is unique. Both Mary and John have the same amount of total connections, 21. Each of them has 9 connections from their Loveline to the Mix [the relationship itself], and each has 12 connections to each other in their Loveline Matrix as we deduced in the last chapter. This is highly unusual to have the same amount of numbers, not just for the entire total, but for both the Loveline Match and Loveline Mix as well.

To have a combined 42 total connections in the Loveline Mix is a large number and signifies there is a great deal of energetic connective tissue between Mary and John. Should their relationship encounter storms of some variety during their life together, they will weather such storms quite nicely. Given all the other connections discussed earlier such as *Soul Release, E-PE Line, Nature Release* and *Polarity Similarity,* the energetic combinations between May and John would garner a very high rating, certainly substantial enough to create a life-long relationship.

Mary and John: Loveline Mix Analysis

Lifepath: Mix 7 [Her 7 LP; his 9 LP]

In most cases, having a 7 show up in the Mix usually indicates some level of spiritual testing, trouble or chaos between the parties involved. This could still be the case, but with the large amount of positive energy in the entire chart, Mary and John should be fine. We all have difficulties in our lives regardless of how perfect a relationship is, and they will have some level of challenge because of this 7 Mix Lifepath.

However, this said, both Mary and John have 7s favorably located in their charts: hers in her Nature and Lifepath; his in his Soul and Material Soul. He loves 7 energy and it's her nature to be all that the 7 represents, so having a 7 Mix Lifepath will not be an uncomfortable energy for them. Both are highly internalized human beings who enjoy their time alone, privacy and reclusion which their Mix 7 LP will give them as a couple. Their life will move them in the direction of study, possibly teaching, philosophy, analysis, examination, metaphysics, religion or spirituality. This is not a life script of business or commercial involvement. It's one reflecting the internal aspects of life.

Expression: Mix 4 [Her 3 Exp.; his 1 Exp.]

This Mix 4 Expression is the only 4 in the Loveline Mix. In this position it means the two will have a strong, secure, grounded, well-defined sense of who they are as a couple. Indications are that they should be quite loyal, dedicated and devoted to each other, the 4 bringing order and constancy to the relationship.

Mary may have some issues with this Mix 4 Expression, however, because her Soul and Material Nature are both 5s. She loves her freedom. She is spontaneous, adventurous, fun, exciting and diverse. The 4 is all about roots, not wings, so she will feel somewhat stifled by their mutual lack of doing new and varied things. John will have to understand this. He has no 5s in his chart, so he's definitely not the adventurous one. Knowing this about Mary will be advantageous for the relationship, especially if they were a couple. In a parent/child relationship, John would find his mother living a more diverse life than he intrinsically understands. As a mother, were Mary aware of these differences, she could, and should, adjust her life to be stable and not so adventure-seeking, especially while her son was growing up. When he's out of the house, that would be a different story, but her first obligation is to her son, not to herself, until he's an adult. If Mary and John are simply good friends, then each can go their own way without expecting too much from the other.

Performance: Mix 2 [Her 1 PE; his 1 PE]

The 2 in the Mix PE position designates a shared life of relationship. When 2 appears in the Mix, it can bring peace or chaos, support or interference, teamwork or adversity, contention or cooperation. Because Mary and John each have 1 energy in their charts, they will have to work at maintaining balance in their relationship, in thinking of each other, supporting each other and sharing. This 2 energy can be good for both of them because not only does it create a life of togetherness, it will force them to be less self-oriented, as their mutual 1 PEs confirm.

Soul: Mix 3 [Her 5 Soul; his 7 Soul]

The Soul energy is not externally active. Still, both Mary and John have strong 3 energy in each of their Lovelines and this 3 Mix Soul will only help to strengthen the overall relationship by creating a solid desire to achieve happiness, joy, pleasure, good times and to be communicative. Whether conscious or subconscious, Mary's Material Soul, Expression and first name will harmonize with this 3 Mix Soul, as will John's Nature and Material Soul.

Material Soul: Mix 1 [Her 3 MS; his 7 MS]

Here we have more harmony for both people. This 1 Mix Material Soul will resonate with both 1 PEs of Mary and John as well as with his 1 Expression. As we know, both individuals are quite independent and this energy will only further that independence and individuality, making the relationship independent as well.

Nature: Mix 1 [Her 7 Nature; his 3 Nature]

More energy of independence. This 1, however, is more active than that in the Mix Material Soul. Other than supporting each person in their individuality, this 1 Mix Nature may possibly create a little friction with the Mix 2 Performance. The numbers 1 and 2 are opposites, so there may be some tug-o-war motion going on in the relationship which will give Mary and John a chance to develop an understanding of togetherness which runs contrary to each of their intrinsic feelings of independence.

Material Nature: Mix 8 [Her 5 MN; his 3 MN]

This adds a different twist to the play that is the life of Mary and John. Eight governs all things external, commercial and socially interactive. Yet, both of them are quite the opposite from a social perspective, given all their mutual and individual 1 and 7 energy. By the same token, this 8 will help balance out the internal aspects of their relationship and force them to integrate, with themselves if not with others. It can also serve to strengthen their external lives by creating a partnership energy of interaction. Therefore, they would do better in public as a couple than as separate people. This Mix 8 Material Nature should give them confidence in social settings which they wouldn't have otherwise.

First Names: Mix 5 [Her 3 of Mary; his 2 of John]

First names are not as powerful as the other components in the Mix but they do have a minor effect. When others emit the words "Mary and John" or "John and Mary," the energy produced is a 5 which activates the 5 energy in Mary's Soul and Material Nature. Because John has no 5s in his Loveline, he won't feel as attached to the "Mary and John" appellation as Mary will. Therefore, she shouldn't be too upset if she notices that he feels differently about "Mary and John" being an item. He's so attracted to her anyway that the first name issue may not be an issue at all.

Rating Guidelines for Attraction and Love

No doubt the question has arisen by now, "How do we rate the attraction and love potential between two people? While there is no precise answer, and other factors in a numerology chart apply, here are some workable Attraction Rating Guidelines.

Powerful Attraction [rare]
1. Both individuals have *Soul Release*.
2. Both individuals have an *Expression to Performance* link.
3. There is at least one *Nature Release* for one partner.
4. Total Mix connections are 35 or higher.
5. Both partners have energies matching the other person in some capacity.
6. Both partners have connections to the Loveline Mix.
7. Strong mirroring of odd or even Loveline numbers.
8. There are no 2s or 7s in the Mix.

Strong Attraction
1. At least one partner has *Soul Release*.
2. At least one partner has an *Expression to Performance*.
3. At least one partner has *Nature Release*.
4. Total Mix connections are 30 or higher.
5. Both partners have energies matching the other person in some capacity.
6. Both partners have connections to the Loveline Mix.
7. Moderate mirroring of odd or even Loveline numbers.
8. A 2 or 7 in the Mix is allowed.

Moderate Attraction

    1. At least one *Soul Release* or *Nature Release* exists in one of the partners.

    2. Total Mix connections are 20 or higher.

    3. Some Loveline matching energies exist.

Little Attraction

    1. No *Releases*.

    2. Some basic connections in the Loveline Mix.

    3. Little to no odd or even numbers in the Mix.

No Attraction

    1. No *Releases*

    2. No basic connections in the Loveline Mix.

    3. Opposing odd and even Loveline energies.

Please keep in mind that these rating guidelines are not cast in stone. They're just indicators and barometers and subject to change as new research dictates. Still, they do give a good idea of what is necessary to generate attraction between individuals and the potential of love growing from that attraction.

Love Mix Templates

Loveline Mix
_____ & _____

		#1	Mix	#2		
External	Lifepath				Lifepath	External
	Expression				Expression	
	P/E				P/E	
Internal	Soul				Soul	Internal
	Material Soul				Material Soul	
	Nature				Nature	
	Material Nature				Material Nature	
	First Name				First Name	

Total Connections: #1 =
Total Connections: #2 =
Total Connections: Mix =

Loveline Mix
_____ & _____

		#1	Mix	#2		
External	Lifepath				Lifepath	External
	Expression				Expression	
	P/E				P/E	
Internal	Soul				Soul	Internal
	Material Soul				Material Soul	
	Nature				Nature	
	Material Nature				Material Nature	
	First Name				First Name	

Total Connections: #1 =
Total Connections: #2 =
Total Connections: Mix =

Chapter Ten

LOVE BUMPS

Love certainly has its bumps. It spite of how perfect a relationship is, this is an imperfect world and there are bound to be imperfections along the road of life. It is a rare person who, having lived long enough, hasn't suffered the pangs of love at some time or another. This chapter addresses a few scenarios that have universal familiarity in the often bumpy road of love.

Unrequited Love

> Ah, Love! How tender, sweet the world 'round;
> It's sovereignty unquestioned and profound;
> But of all the hurts and weeping raining down,
> Unrequited love displays the crown.

Arguably, there is no pain more painful or hurt more hurtful than an aching heart torn apart because its love is unreturned. "Why," we may ask, "doesn't the heart I love so much love me back?" Sometimes, unfortunately, it can't. As we've been studying, love and attraction are a function of energy, energy defined by numbers, and if the energies between two people do not harmonize, even though one person desperately loves the other, love between the two just can't materialize. Hence, love will go unrequited, unreturned, unacknowledged, unrealized.

The following hypothetical Loveline Matrix shows why.

Unrequited Love: Loveline Match

	Person #1	Lovelines		Person # 2	
External	Lifepath	7	9	Lifepath	External
	Expression	7	8	Expression	
	P/E	5	8	P/E	
Internal	Soul	8	8	Soul	Internal
	Material Soul	6	8	Material Soul	
	Nature	6	9	Nature	
	Material Nature	4	9	Material Nature	
	First Name	5	2	First Name	

In this Unrequited Loveline Match example, the 8 Soul of Person #1 is helplessly drawn to the enormous amount of 8 energy in Person #2. It is the Soul, the individual's core, that defines the needs, wants, desires and intrinsic motivations of a person. So here we have the most primal core needs of Person #1 naturally magnetized to Person #2's Expression, PE, Soul and Material Soul. Person #1 will absolutely feel great attraction for practically all that Person #2 is and may wonder why there is no returned love.

Unfortunately, even though Person #2 may well appreciate the adoration from Person #1 and sense Person #1's attraction, and even though the Souls match [8], Person #2's Soul has no release though the Loveline of Person #1. In fact, the Lifepath and Expression of Person #1 are both 7s, the exact opposite of Person #2's 8 Soul, Material Soul, Expression and PE - practically the entire makeup of the person. Therefore, right away we can see this isn't going to work.

Another reason why this relationship will be bumpy is in the Loveline Mix.

Unrequited Love: Loveline Mix

		#1	Mix	#2		
External	Lifepath	7	7	9	Lifepath	External
	Expression	7	6	8	Expression	
	P/E	5	4	8	P/E	
Internal	Soul	8	7	8	Soul	Internal
	Material Soul	6	5	8	Material Soul	
	Nature	6	6	9	Nature	
	Material Nature	4	4	9	Material Nature	
	First Name	5	7	2	First Name	

Notice the three 7s in the Mix. Generally, as explained earlier, 7s in the Mix portend challenges and trouble in the relationship. In this case, those areas of concern will be in the Mix Lifepath, Soul and First Name components, the Lifepath being the most problematic. Neither Person #1 or #2 will be comfortable with this 7 amalgam because it runs counter to what each wants, as depicted by their individual 8 Soul energies. Person #2 will absolutely not feel any attraction because of this 7 grouping. Person #1 will feel it more, especially in the unrequited love sense. Not only is the 7 Lifepath spiritually challenging, as all 7 Lifepaths can be, but to pursue such a relationship would not be wise because it would only magnify the potential heartache caused by the 7 energy in the Mix, especially in the Lifepath. Were this relationship to somehow come together, Person #1 would be happy for a time. Person #2 would like being worshipped, but it would all come crashing down in time.

Therefore, in assessing the attraction/love quotient, always check the *Soul Release* first. It is the most critical aspect in determining the breadth, depth, scope and ultimate success of any relationship, whatever its structure. Also consider the balance of energies between the parties involved. Lopsided energies, as in the example above, will not create positive relationship outcomes.

The Love/Hate Debate

There's no question unrequited love is tough. Perhaps equally as tough, but certainly more exasperating, is when two people are attracted to each other, love each other, but are constantly engaged in endless turmoil. Our example indicates such challenges.

Love/Hate: Loveline Mix

		#1	Mix	#2		
External	Lifepath	7	9	2	Lifepath	External
	Expression	4	7	3	Expression	
	P/E	2	7	5	P/E	
Internal	Soul	3	7	4	Soul	Internal
	Material Soul	1	7	6	Material Soul	
	Nature	1	9	8	Nature	
	Material Nature	8	9	1	Material Nature	
	First Name	7	7	9	First Name	

How do we know there's attraction between these two? If you noticed the mutual *Soul Release* you're right on the ball. Person #1 has a 3 Soul which finds release through the 3 Expression of #2, whose 4 Soul finds its own release through the 4 Expression of #1.

In effect, each person desires the other. Additionally, the 1 Material Soul and 1 Nature of Person #1 resonate with the 1 Material Nature of Person #2. The 8 Nature of Person #2 matches the 8 Material Nature of Person #1. These connections create definite attractions.

However, even though there is some noticeable magnetism, the turmoil is in the Mix, just as "the devil is in the details." Look at all those 7s! Because of the little amount of 7 energy in their individual Lovelines [which would generate some resonance], the painful amount of Mix 7 energy is heart wrenching. Even though these two people have a mutual and positive attraction, their lives, unfortunately, create a mutual and negative distraction in the form of intrinsic turmoil . . . and a lot of it.

This example illustrates why it's important to always check the Mix when assessing a relationship. Comparing only Lovelines is simply not enough. People could be desperately in love with each other but incapable of being with each other because of the chaos created by their intertwining energies.

Tug-O-War Love

Ever seen an ostensibly awesome relationship where there is a constant tugging back and forth between the parties, where there is a strong connection and attraction but also simultaneous harmony and inharmony; where each of the partners is so alike one would think their relationship would be perfect but somehow it just doesn't garner a "perfect rating?" The following is one example of how this may occur.

Tug-O-War: Loveline Mix

		#1	Mix	#2		
External	Lifepath	9	9	9	Lifepath	External
	Expression	1	2	1	Expression	
	P/E	1	2	1	P/E	
Internal	Soul	1	2	1	Soul	Internal
	Material Soul	1	2	1	Material Soul	
	Nature	9	9	9	Nature	
	Material Nature	9	9	9	Material Nature	
	First Name	1	2	1	First Name	

If one were to only assess the Loveline Match between these two people, it would seem really good, and for most accounts, it is. There is mutual *Soul Release* and *Material Soul Release*. In fact, in both partners these releases are doubled because they harmonize with both the Expression and the PE of the partner. Plus, they both have an Expression to Performance. Wow! This is awesome. They share the same Nature and Material Nature, too. Life and love are good, sort of.

The main area of concern here is the vast amount of 2 energy in the Mix versus the vast amount of 1 energy in the Lovelines. This creates a two-edged sword which these people may live and die by [figuratively]. The number 2 rules both war and peace; balance and imbalance; allies and adversaries; up and down; back and forth; teeter-tottering vacillation. You get the picture. Therefore, these two people will have to learn to balance their powerful egos and personal ambitions in deference to their relationship as well as the other person and their ambitions. They each have enormous energy of self and ego but their relationship is forcing them to consider the other person, not themselves - quite a dilemma.

In effect, this is one example of numerical cloning. Both people are mirrors of each other. There's no chaos between them, which 7 energy would create, but there is a humongous amount of energy related to ego, power and tug-o-warring. Furthermore, the numbers 1 and 2 are direct opposites. The number 1 rules the self; the 2, others; 1 is fire, 2 is water; 1 is male, 2 is female; 1 is reason, 2 is emotion; 1 is the leader, 2 is the follower.

Both of these people are ego-centric, self-oriented, self-motivating, strong willed. Their lives are all about themselves, as is clearly evident in their 1 Souls and Material Souls. Furthermore, this is corroborated by their 1 Expressions, 1 PEs and First Names. To make matters worse, their mutual 9 Natures, Material Natures and Lifepaths generate even more power. No two numbers together are more dominant and powerful than the 1 and 9.

But here's the rub: their Mix is all 2s and 9s - relationship and rulership. In a way, these two people deserve each other, but can their relationship, as connective as it is, withstand the battles and power struggles their egos create? With so much 1 energy, can each of them subordinate their mutually dense pelf of self to their relationship which is marked by the number 2, an energy neither of them has in their Loveline? Such involvements create an intense tug-o-war like no other. Either these people will learn to get along and embrace the strength and individuality in the other and the togetherness of their partnership or they'll decide to go their own ways in spite of their mutual attraction, shaking their heads in bewilderment as to why their seemingly perfect relationship didn't, or couldn't, work.

Roots & Scoots

No number loves its roots more than the 4. No number loves to scoot and move more than the 5. The 4 is conventional; the 5 is non-conventional. The 4 is cautious; the 5 is adventurous. The 4 craves security; the 5 will forego security to preserve its freedom. The 4 is ruled by earth; the 5 by fire. When these two connect in love, their union will be one of potential frustration hopefully leading to adjustments on both ends in the realm of give-and-take.

Roots & Scoots: Loveline Mix

		#1	Mix	#2		
External	Lifepath	4	9	5	Lifepath	External
	Expression	4	9	5	Expression	
	P/E	8	9	1	P/E	
Internal	Soul	5	9	4	Soul	Internal
	Material Soul	9	9	9	Material Soul	
	Nature	8	9	1	Nature	
	Material Nature	3	9	6	Material Nature	
	First Name	5	9	4	First Name	

There is much attraction between these two individuals. Both share *Soul Release* through the other's Expression, a powerful connection as we know. Person #2's 4 Soul matches Person #1's 4 LP and Expression. Likewise, person #1's 5 Soul matches Person #2's 5 LP and Expression. The 5 First Name of Person #1 also harmonizes with the 5 Lifepath and Expression of Person #2. The 4 First Name of Person #2 also resonates with the 4 Lifepath and 4 Expression of Person #1. All this is good.

Still, there are love bumps here. The Lifepaths, Expressions, Souls and First Names exist in opposition to the other person. The result, a "Roots versus Scoots" engagement with the 4 advocating all that is stable, secure, conventional, practical and reasonable while the 5 argues for excitement, freedom, motion, movement, diversity, spontaneity and adventure. There is no great contention in the Mix as noted by the absence of 2 and 7 energy, but there are power struggles and issues clearly evident not only in the oppositional 4 versus 5 arena but also in the complete Loveline Mix of 9 energy of power and dominance, a most rare occurrence.

This Loveline Mix saturation of 9 energy indicates the extreme universality, power and public persona of this relationship. The #2 individual supplies the leadership, direction and adventure, as noted by the 1 and 5 energy respectively, while the #1 person supports their 9 based union with organization and management indicated by the 4 and 8 energy respectively. It's a very unique bond of opposites which bring together opposing energies [the 4 and 5] to create a universal energy entity of completeness and power [9]. Were a relationship such as this to endure, it would be quite interesting to see how each person managed the other's opposing characteristics. Perhaps the inherent love in the relationship offers enough glue to keep it together and fruitful. The key to making this relationship work would be for each partner to agree to do what one person wants one day and then to do what the other person wants to do on another day. In other words, compromise. For the 4 to remain rigid and demand constant practicality, or for the 5 to insist on spontaneity and endless adventure, would only generate relentless tension and opposition. Love demands surrender, sacrifice, adjustment and accommodation and, in fact, a true lover would want to compromise and insure the happiness of his or her partner.

Conflicted 8 Mates

In this scenario, we see two people who are socially powerful in their worlds, vis-à-vis their 8 Expressions and 8 Natures, which are corroborated by their 9 Souls. The numbers 8 and 9 together create a potent duo of social power. Both of these individuals are ambitious and driven to seek the public stage [9 Soul], while expressing their social, managerial and executive skills through their 8 energy. Each has some internal release: Person #1 has an 8 *Nature Release* through the 8 Expression of Person #2, as well as a 4 *Material Nature Release* through the 4 Lifepath of Person #2. Person #2 has a 4 *Material Soul Release* through the 4 PE of Person #1, as well as an 8 *Nature Release* through the 8 Expression and 8 Nature of Person #1. Both have 9 Soul release through their 9 Mix Lifepath which is strengthened by the 9 energies in the Soul categories of the Lovelines. Attraction exists.

Conflicted 8 Mates: Loveline Mix

		#1	Mix	#2		
External	Lifepath	5	9	4	Lifepath	External
	Expression	8	7	8	Expression	
	P/E	4	7	3	P/E	
Internal	Soul	9	9	9	Soul	Internal
	Material Soul	5	9	4	Material Soul	
	Nature	8	7	8	Nature	
	Material Nature	4	7	3	Material Nature	
	First Name	5	2	6	First Name	

The love bump between these two lies in the large amount of 7 Mix energy in the Expression, PE, Nature and Material Nature - 7 energy that is directly opposite from their mutual 8 Expressions and mutual 8 Natures. These two can socialize with others quite well, but being together is another story. There's distance between them, a coldness and aloofness that a person on the outside may not see. In fact, there could even be a great deal of turmoil in their lives. These two, although sharing an intrinsic attraction for each other, create chaos, making them very conflicted mates. This relationship could easily fall into the love/hate category as well. It is also a good example of why it's not a good thing to necessarily have a relationship with someone who's very much like yourself. Clones are susceptible to confliction in one way or another.

These few examples we've studied are hypothetical. Yet, they serve to illustrate that although attraction and love can exist between two people based on their Loveline Matrix, their relationship may be colored by their Loveline Mix which may create some love bumps and challenges along the way. To be sure, this is a duality-based dimension where light and darkness co-exist. For those in love, it is wise to remember that relationships take work, sacrifice, commitment and surrender to the relationship itself; that neither partner is more important than the other, and that to build a positive union, balance and understanding are a critical ingredient to the relationship and wholeness of the parties involved.

Chapter Eleven

LOVE VOIDS

Voids are missing letters and their corresponding numbers in the full birth name. In the Simple Letter Value Chart, each of the single numbers 1 through 9 is associated with different letter groupings called *genera*. The number 1, for example, is associated with the A-J-S genera; the number 2 is related to the B-K-T genera and so forth. When any of these letter classes is absent in a natal name, there is a *void*, a numerical vacancy, an empty vibration. If a person has a 9 void, there are no Is or Rs in the name. If a person has a 4 void, there are no Ds, Ms or Vs in the name.

Simple Letter Value Chart									
The Letters	A	B	C	D	E	F	G	H	I
	J	K	L	M	N	O	P	Q	R
	S	T	U	V	W	X	Y	Z	
Number Value	1	2	3	4	5	6	7	8	9

If a voided number is also absent in any component of the Loveline, it is called a *Grand Void*. For example, an individual with a 3 void [no Cs, Ls or Us in the birth name], as well as no 3s in the Loveline [Basic Matrix] is said to have a 3 *Grand Void*.

Void Analogies

There are several ways we can look at voids. First, we can think of voids as a lack of construction tools. For example, if a carpenter were to begin building a house but had no saw to cut the wood needed to construct the dwelling, he would obviously have a void, not only in his tool chest (the missing saw) but a void in his ability to perform his job. If a writer wanted to create a book but had little or no understanding of words, he, too, would suffer a void, for words are the tools of the writer. If a parent lacked an understanding of structure, the importance of discipline and establishing foundations in a child's life - important tools in building solid, responsible and whole children - he or she, too, would suffer a void. Voids reflect absences of skill, substance and ability.

A second analogy is to see voids as missing "sacks on the back." For example, let's picture a person, like a hobo, journeying through life carrying nine small sacks on his back - nine thin numbered sticks extending over his shoulder each with a small sack or kerchief attached to its end and holding some contents except, in this case, the contents of each sack are the single numbers 1-2-3-4-5-6-7-8-9 matching the numbers of each stick. Each number, of course, represents qualities the individual will need to manage his life. If the number 1 stick has no contents in its sack or kerchief, the individual has a 1 void. If the number 6 sack/kerchief is empty, he has a 6 void. If any of the sacks/kerchiefs are empty, the individual will be lacking those particular skills and attributes [creating a void] as he traverses the path of his life.

A third analogy is that of wiring in which each of the nine basic numbers 1-2-3-4-5-6-7-8-9 represents the composite "wiring" of the individual. Each number, as a wire, manifests specific characteristics and attributes across which flow specific energies allowing the individual to operate as a conscious living being. When an individual's full natal name houses all of the single numbers, his wiring is complete and his ability to operate as a balanced, harmonious and functionally integrated human being are enhanced. When a number or numbers are missing in the chart, the wiring is incomplete and the individual's chances of living a full, whole, balanced and effective life are comprised.

Think of an automobile and its structure. It is filled with all kinds of wires which send mechanical or electrical signals to its various parts, thus allowing the car to run smoothly and efficiently. For example, assume the ignition system has no wiring. The car couldn't start even if the remainder of the car's wiring were complete. Perhaps the ignition system is in tact but there are no break lines from the brake pedal to the wheels. The car will not be able to stop even if it gets moving. If there's no wiring from the steering column to the front end wheel assembly, the car may be able to start, it may be able to go, it may be able to stop but it won't be able to turn. Obviously then, an automobile's wiring system is critical to its health, integration and functionability. Without all of the wiring in tact, an automobile may not only be inefficient but dangerous . . . to itself and others.

So it is with people. If their wiring is complete, their lives and happiness will be potentially enhanced. If their wiring is lacking, they will be lacking, their lives manifesting potential problems and causing possible disruption to themselves and others.

A fourth analogy of voids is that they're just holes in the armor of an individual's being or, if one prefers, chinks in the armor of one's personal defenses. In the battle of life, we all need defenses to protect us from the aggressive attacks of predators, whether they're assaulting the physical, financial, professional, personal, emotional, psychological or spiritual components of our being. No one in their right mind would think of entering a nuclear reactor chamber with hole-ridded protective clothing, or spending extended time in the sun without sunscreen, or working in a construction zone without a helmet, boots, gloves and the correct type of clothing.

Voids - whether we see them as an absence of tools, sacks, wiring, armor or protective clothing - are critical factors relating to our life, especially to our relationships. In lieu of the nature of voids, it would be wise to consider their effects in a person's life or relationships.

Most of us have a void or voids in our chart. It's normal to have them, but the more voids we have, the more potential problems and challenges we may have in life. Having voids doesn't mean we are a bad person. Many great souls have had voids. General George Patton and Marilyn Monroe [born Norma Jeane Mortenson] had a 3 void in their charts. Mother Teresa maintained a 4 void in her chart. Amelia Earhart, Charles Lindberg, Martin Luther King, Helen Keller and William Shakespeare all had a 6 void. Abraham Lincoln, Albert Einstein, Albert Schweitzer, Charles Darwin and Helen Keller had a 7 void.

Having voids simply means we will have issues with those areas associated with the voided number(s).

How Voids Manifest Themselves

How do voids manifest themselves? Usually in one of three ways:

1. The individual will totally ignore its energy and characteristics. For example, a person with a 2 void may have absolutely no concern or regard for others and their well-being or for close personal relationships.

2. The person will do everything he can to try and fill the void(s), even over-compensate by totally involving himself in the conditions which the void represents. For example, many people with a Six (6) void may spend their lives trying to find love and romance while others with a 6 void may have little or no concern about a home or domestic life.

3. The person will display the negative aspects of the number involved. In the case of the number Six, the person may become a firestorm of hate, jealousy, animosity, anger or envy. An individual with a 7 void may become secretly treacherous, foolish and ignoble with a cold and calculating approach to life and people.

Void Chart

The following Void Chart details the assortment of issues a person may have with a particular void. For example, a person with a 1 void will have potential issues with his self-confidence and self-worth, personal image and identity, independence, etc.

Void Chart

Void	General Description - Issues Involving:
1 A-J-S	The self and its worth, independence, the Yang--male influence, male principles, male figures, fathers, brothers, bosses, leaders, managers, action, leadership, creativity, ego, self-esteem, taking charge, standing up for one's self, being alone, drive, ambition, direction.
2 B-K-T	Others, relationships, the Yin--female influence, female principles, female figures, mothers, sisters, following and being the follower, supporting and being the supporter, balance, receptivity, sensitivity, tolerance, caring, helping, sharing, diplomacy, deceit, duplicity, indirectness, intuition, close personal relationships.
3 C-L-U	Self-expression, health, beauty, personal integration, marriage, children, speech, friends, words, happiness, joy, ease, disease, dis-ease, communication, harshness of expression, criticism, vanity.
4 D-M-V	All things of structure and order, work, effort, control, roots, discipline, regimentation, details, clerical, understanding, security, service, rules, regulations, duty, devotion, fidelity, honesty, trust, strength, safety.
5 E-N-W	Freedom, change, people in general, movement, experience, talents, variety, the senses, sex, crowds, activity, excitement, exploration, shifting, uncertainty, wildness, intemperate, unrestrained, undisciplined, out of control, enslavement.
6 F-O-X	Matters of the home, heart and hearth, domesticity, family, love, sex, romance, compassion, balance, beauty, harmony, community, personal responsibility and accountability, honoring, adjustment.
7 G-P-Y	Inner peace, spirituality, mysticism, religion, inquisition, insight, being alone, alienation, isolation, separation, privacy, reflection, poise, perfection, depth of being, thoughtfulness, concern, calm, chaos,

		confusion, nobility, ignobility, thoughtlessness, coldness, cruelty, ruthlessness, indifference, secretive, inconsiderate, withdrawing, receding, recession, wisdom.
	8 **H-Q-Z**	Interaction, connection, disconnection, continuity, flow, business, commerce, worldly status, management, executive leadership, wealth, success, material power, riches, comfort, administration, manipulation, orchestration, marketing, usury, being in the loop.
	9 **I-R**	Universality, compassion, strength, power, rulership, respect for others, service, understanding of the 'all', the 'many', the macrocosm, impersonal love, comprehensive feeling, arrogance, dominance, being over-bearing, impudent, rude, imperious, malevolence, benevolence, broadcasting, recognition.

Managing the Spectrum of Voids

1 Void

If we have 1 void, we need to concentrate on and work toward being whole and independent without being egocentric, arrogant and self-absorbed. A 1 voided person would be well-served in being patient with authority figures but not allowing others to dominate him or do for him. A 1 void demands we do things for ourselves, stand on our own two feet as well as standing up and being counted, being strong and courageous. It also means we must learn to be direct and forthright in our dealings with others, as well as being able to look at our faults, failings and shortcomings and not point the finger of blame on others. A 1 void can make a person very empty but dangerous. People lacking self worth often attempt to cut others down to build themselves up - a tactic that only further impacts them negatively. The 1 rules male energy and therefore male issues, and males in general will be associated with a 1 void. Ego, self and Yang issues will be exacerbated when the 1 occupies a Challenge position [see *The King's Book of Numerology II: Forecasting - Part I*]. Incidentally, when 1 is in any Challenge timeline whether it is voided or not, problems with the ego or males and their accompanying issues loom large, so one is cautioned to be ever vigilant if possible in keeping yang attributes in check, lest their fires run rampant, destroying them and others in the process.

2 Void

Two rules the female. Two also rules others, close interpersonal relationships, partnerships, diplomacy, tact, caring, helping, support, competition, togetherness, division, conflict, war, balance and peace. Therefore, a person with a 2 void must learn to be the helper, supporter, peace-maker, diplomat, friend, team player, partner and business associate. Women will also be a challenge, especially if the 2 occupies a Challenge timeline. This would include mothers, mothers-in-law, grandmothers, sisters, aunts, female friends and associates. A Two void could be difficult for a person with a large amount of 1 energy because the 1 focuses on himself, not others; independence, not dependence; leading not following; hoarding, not sharing. A 2 voided individual must be cautious of ignoring others or even violating their right to life and happiness. A 2 void often causes great stress in close relationships. To overcome such a void, the individual should concentrate on balance and seeing life from the other person's point of view.

3 Void

Three rules life, its abundance, joy, children, health, happiness, pleasure, words, speech, art, sex and self-expression. A person with a 3 void needs to focus on being positive, healthy and avoid habits and activities that interfere with or destroy health or well-being - his own or other people's. Oftentimes, a 3 voided challenge equates to harshness and meanness in words and actions. People with a 3 void can be plagued with unhappiness, as is well-documented in the life of Marilyn Monroe [born Norma Jeane Mortenson], a soul who was constantly in search of finding contentment and joy in her life. George Patton is an excellent example of a person who tried to fill the void of the 3. He was a voracious reader, but, by some accounts, vain. Because 3 rules beauty, one of the dangers is vanity and an over-exaggeration with one's self-image or in some cases, no image. History has proven that both Monroe and Patton had image issues that bordered on, or translated into, vanity. Three also rules children and it's not uncommon for women with a 3 void or voided challenge to be barren or have no desire whatsoever to have children, even like them. A 3 voided person needs to concentrate of being positive and grateful for everything . . . even if "everything" is not what the person wants. This will allow the individual to avoid the great sin of ingratitude, which may well be why the person was given the void in the first place.

4 Void

Four governs order, organization, design, building, construction, destruction, structure, routines, regimens, service, matter, limitation, restriction, protection, security, loyalty, fidelity, discipline, control, mechanics, patterns, honesty and trust. Therefore, when Four is void there exist potential problems in any of these areas. When Four is a Voided Challenge or a Grand Voided Challenge [see *The King's Book of Numerology II: Forecasting - Part I*], the issues become intense. Faithlessness, infidelity and dishonesty loom large, as does a person's personal security and safety. It's difficult to be organized with no organizational skills, no discipline, no self-control. Four in a Challenge position can also make one feel as though he is imprisoned. This is because of the 4's propensity to confine, constrict, restrict and limit.

Other scenarios exist for this structure-oriented cipher. For example, a person with a 4v/3 may well have no code of morals or ethics to live by, engaging in excessive sensual pleasures, lies and unkindnesses and possessing a mean-spirited, vindictive attitude. With this 4v/3 pattern, a woman may be barren of children since the 4 is besieged with a lack of structure playing itself out in the realm of children (3). Four rules matter and the material body, so when it is void it follows that there will be issues of bodily strength, security and wholeness. Finding happiness will be challenging in this 4v/3 IR set and overall health issues will be a major concern if this dyad is located in a Challenge position. Pythagoras said, "No man is free who cannot control himself," and so a lack of 4 energy could result in a loss of freedom to some extent.

Another caution for the 4 void is to avoid being too resistant, stubborn and recalcitrant. Being strong is one thing, but being unruly and antagonistic may create a dangerous and unhealthy rigidity.

5 Void

It's vary rare to have a 5 void because "E" is the most used letter in the English language and "N" is also very common. Having no 5s would affect a person's sense of movement, freedom and ability to change. If 5 is voided or challenged, drastic change, uncertainty and loss are quite possible. This is because one of the binary roots of the 5 is the 14, the cipher of loss and detachment. Five not only rules freedom but also slavery, the opposite side of its coin. Coupled with 4 energy, a person could easily find himself stuck in a rut, a ship anchored securely in place with no compunction to move, explore or be free.

A lack of 5 energy may over-stimulate a person to experience a wide array of sensations, involvement in deleterious substances such as drugs and alcohol and seek a profligate, promiscuous lifestyle. The 5 rules curiosity, and remember what curiosity did to the cat . . . it killed it. 5 also rules speed, so one must be careful not to move too fast, lest one lose total control of himself. Speed kills - in more ways than one. A 5 voided person would be well-advised to be temperate, controlled and use discretion to all things. While freedom is wonderful, its flip side is slavery, and countless people have become enslaved to the very things in which they "freely" indulged. The truth is, nothing is free; everything has a price, and too much of any worldly thing is not a good thing. Freedom - true freedom - demands discipline, discretion, self-control and enough forethought to look ahead to the consequences of one's actions before those actions are taken. Once the arrow is let loose or the trigger pulled, neither the arrow nor the bullet can be retrieved. Acting without first thinking is a recipe for disaster.

6 Void

Six voids herald problems and issues with domestic matters, love, nurturing, family, heart, home and romance. It's not uncommon for famous people to have a 6 void. Einstein, Schweitzer, Shakespeare, Earhart, Lindbergh, Helen Keller and Martin Luther King, Jr. all possessed this missing cipher in their names. Yet, they were extremely successful in their fields of endeavor, leading one to surmise that perhaps if God wants a soul to dedicate itself to some line of work and not be anchored to the home, He gives it a 6 void, thus limiting its involvement in a home life and allowing for more devotion to other endeavors. It is a fact, however, that if a 6 is in a Grand Voided Challenge position, there will be extreme difficulties in the home life and in the heart. There will be a lack of love, nurturing, harmony and peace within the domicile. Adjustments and responsibilities could easily be major issues. The 6 Voided Challenge is all about love and/or the lack of it. The Six void also carries the potential concentration of its polar aspects - hate, envy, jealousy, bitterness, resentment. It could also be manifested in a person who has responsibility for the home as a caretaker, gardener, butler, maid, servant, attending spouse for a sick or ailing partner or family member.

Regardless of the degree, a 6 void will engage the individual in some facet of the love life, heart, domestic environment or community habitat. The solution to the heartache is to be loving, not angry for not having love; to be nurturing, caring, sympathetic and loyal so as not to plant negative seeds that will eventually grow to fruition at some future time, creating more heartache or familial frustration.

<u>7 Void</u>

The main problem with the Seven void is depth of thought, or rather the lack of it. This 7 void can make one inconsiderate, indifferent, cold, distant, detached, even ruthless. Seven rules all things internal, especially those dealing with the mind and spirit. The perfect statuesque symbol for the Seven is Rodin's Thinker, ever posed in deep thought with his head resting on his hand, supported by his arm on his knee. Thus, no 7, no deep thinking, no wisdom, at least on one side of its coin. The irony is that, as we've discussed, one way voids are managed is that the person tries to fill them with the exact energy of the void. For example, Abraham Lincoln was, arguably, the greatest president in United States history and an extremely deep thinker. Yet, he maintained a 7 void, as did Helen Keller, Albert Einstein, Albert Schweitzer, Charles Darwin, Jackie Robinson and Marilyn Monroe, although many of these people did have 7s in their Loveline/Basic Matrix. It's as if the lack of 7 energy drives the individual to fill himself up with it.

Another issue with the 7 void is the ability to be still and calm since 7 rules peace and quiet. We know Lincoln had suffered from depression and despondency from time to time. Was this breakdown a manifestation of his 7 void? Helen Keller also had stillness issues, especially when she was young. The moral of this story, as it is with all voids - recognize that the polar differences within each number can and do manifest themselves in completely opposite ways. Every coin has two sides; every cloud has a silver lining; every night has its day. Seek, therefore, the positive to nullify the negative and bring balance into the life.

8 Void

Eight rules flow and connection. It is the conduit of the numeric spectrum. When 8 is void, there is no flow, no connection, no conduit. Hence, things do not go smoothly or run efficiently. To have, for example, a person in a management or administrative position with an 8 void and no 8s in the Basic Matrix, let alone having the 8 possibly be situated as a Voided Challenge or Grand Voided Challenge in one of the P/C timelines, is tantamount to financial ruin and commercial disaster. In order for things to flow properly, one must be able to connect idea to manifestation, concept to completion, product to sale, buyer to seller. It is the 8 that allows this to happen. Worldly success has often been associated with the 8, and the reason for this is the 8's inherent capacity to connect the dots and get things done. Without an 8 in the mix, things don't get done efficiently because the energy's not there to make it happen. A person with no 8s simply can't see how to connect or integrate, how to go from point A to point B. Eight is the great administrator and coordinator. Eight is also the great manipulator (remember, every number has a positive and negative aspect). Eight is equally applauded by crooks and gods alike. With 8s present in a chart, probabilities of success exist; without 8s, the outlook is slim to none that success will be a reality.

Two problems of which to be aware with the 8 void are non-responsiveness and procrastination. 8 is the highest and most powerful social vibration and when it's absent, people tend to have issues with being responsive to others and procrastinate when they should be being about the task at hand. Therefore, the 8 void person must concentrate on being responsive and efficient.

Being non-responsive tends to make people indifferent to others, especially on a personal level. Few things destroy or kill a relationship faster or more efficiently than indifference. When 8 is void, there is no connection, no support. A total absence of feelings, sympathy, empathy or involvement in and for the lives of other individuals often occurs. People just don't care about others on a deep level when the connective vibratory tissue of the 8 is absent. Such people may be popular based on other energies in the chart such as a 3 or 9, but on an intimately personal level, there's little concern or endearment for others.

An 8 void is often present in the charts of criminals and predators, who may be superficially charismatic in order to lure their victims, but who have absolutely no regard for their prey. If they cared for others, they wouldn't be predators in the first place. Two extremely infamous characters are notorious mass-murderer Charles Manson [birth name: "No Name Maddox"] and master fraud schemer, Bernie Madoff [birth name: "Bernard Lawrence Madoff"]. Neither of these decrepit souls had any concern for the people whose lives they destroyed. Too, in conjunction with their 8 voids, they both had a 7 void in their charts. The "7 void/8 void" combination is arguably the worst and most nefariously problematic ciphered compound there is. It's potentially ice cold and heartless.

Let's be clear: not all people with a 7 void and 8 void are evil. There are many factors in a chart to consider when making assessments, but one would be wise to take note of such potentials and not ignore them.

<u>9 Void</u>

Nine governs the public stage, theater, humanity, expansion, exposure, arts, education, fame, notoriety, endings, terminations, conclusions, resolutions, travel, respect for others, recognition, triumph and universality. Nine is the great giver, albeit an impersonal one, or the great taker, without a doubt a heartless and remorseless one. Because 9 rules the public/global stage, it is highly unusual for a person to be known by the masses without it. Nine exposes, expands, recognizes and broadcasts. Regardless of one's talents, without a 9 in the chart, notoriety will most likely never occur. This is obvious by studying the charts of famous people. Inevitably, they all have 9 somewhere in their numbers. It would be impossible to touch the public without it. The 9 void may cause people to seek the limelight or work with humanity in some manner, especially in a volunteer capacity. Nine in a Pinnacle or Challenge position [see *The King's Book of Numerology II: Forecasting - Part I*] will most likely generate travel on some level - physically, psychologically, spiritually. Without a 9 present in a chart, an individual will have a difficult time connecting with or being associated with the masses, that is unless he tries to fill his life with them.

With a 9 void it's not uncommon for a person to be involved with the public in some capacity, even to be anti-public. To what degree and in what aspect [positive or negative] depends on other numbers and factors in the chart. A 9 void often manifests by the person not having a full grasp of the big picture or having little to no respect for others and their lives and pursuits. It can also cause one to perform untoward actions in order to gain public recognition or acceptance. If a person craves acknowledgement beyond the norm and is denied such recognition, then negative circumstances can arise. To be acknowledged, it is important to acknowledge, so the solution for a lack of acknowledgment is to acknowledge and recognize others first, be generally happy for them and their success. This will plant good seed which, by natural law, must one day grow to fruition and bless the sower with an abundant harvest.

Mary & John: Voids

Let's now take a look at the chart of Mary Jane Smith and John David Doey to determine if they have any voids in their charts.

<u>Mary Jane Smith: Voids 3 & 6</u>

M	A	R	Y	J	A	N	E	S	M	I	T	H
4	1	9	7	1	1	5	5	1	4	9	2	8

No 3s or 6s present
The Voids of Mary Jane Smith are: 3 & 6

By assessing the numbers associated with each of the letters in Mary's natal name, we see that she has no Cs, Ls or Us representing the 3 energy; nor does she have any Fs, Os or Xs, the energy of the 6. All the other numbers between 1 and 9 are accounted for. Therefore, Mary's voids are 3 & 6. When we check her Loveline, we see she does have a 3 in her Expression and Material Soul. This is a good thing. It keeps her from having a Grand Voided 3 which would potentially be more problematic than a simple 3 void.

Loveline of Mary Jane Smith: Born 8 January 1960

Mary Jane Smith: Born 8 January 1960	
Lifepath	7
Expression	**3**
Performance	1
Soul	5
Material Soul	**3**
Nature	7
Material Nature	5

The 3 void indicates Mary will potentially have challenges, issues, concerns or problems with her self-expression, image, words, communication skills, health, pleasure. This should not be too severe, however, because her 3 Expression makes her the epitome of the 3 energy itself. Too, her Material Soul of 3 gives her a desire to seek and give pleasure, happiness, joy to others, as well as being a good communicator. Given the combination of her 7 Lifepath, 7 Nature and 1 PE, she may well love to write or create with her mind in some capacity.

Mary's 6 void is, in fact, a 6 Grand Void because she has no 6s in her Loveline. Mary will definitely experience issues relating to love, romance, the home, heart and hearth, nurturing, supporting and being domestically oriented. When we assess her Loveline Mix with John, there are no 6s present at all between them. Thus, we can surmise that love, in some capacity, will be an issue for Mary throughout her life. Given this reality of the 6 Grand Void, she may totally neglect the 6 energy, perhaps giving time to a professional career, finding happiness and fulfillment in her work rather than in a family environment. She may try to fill the 6 void with multiple love affairs, or she may exhibit anger as an outpouring of frustration. By analyzing her *Life Matrix* [see *The King's Book of Numerology II: Forecasting - Part I*], we could easily assess the extent to which the 6 would or would not be problematic in her life - a subject for further study.

John David Doey: Voids 2 & 3

John's natal name has no Bs, Ks or Ts, thus creating a 2 void. He also has no Cs, Ls or Us, giving him an additional void of 3. His Loveline does have 3s, a good thing. Yet, he is absent a 2 in his Basic Matrix, making John's 2 a Grand Void. Thus, John will have issues, challenges, concerns and potential problems with close personal relationships, others, female energy, finding balance in his life, being a team player, supporter and partner.

J	O	H	N	D	A	V	I	D	D	O	E	Y
1	6	8	5	4	1	4	9	4	4	6	5	7

No 2s or 3s present
The Voids of John David Doey are: 2 & 3

Loveline of John David Doey: Born 14 August 1985

John David Doey Born 14 August 1985	
Lifepath	9
Expression	1
Performance	1
Soul	7
Material Soul	7
Nature	3
Material Nature	3

One of the saving graces in John's chart is that his relationship with Mary will be of great value to him. Mary has 2 energy in her name [the "T" of "Smith"] and the Mix between her and John manifests a 2 PE. Therefore, John will gravitate not only to Mary but to their relationship, as it fills the 2 void energy he's missing in his life.

Loveline Mix: Mary and John

		Mary	#1	Mix	#2	John	
External		Lifepath	7	7	9	Lifepath	External
		Expression	3	4	1	Expression	
		P/E	1	2	1	P/E	
Internal		Soul	5	3	7	Soul	Internal
		Material Soul	3	1	7	Material Soul	
		Nature	7	1	3	Nature	
		Material Nature	5	8	3	Material Nature	
		First Name	3	5	2	First Name	

Void Summary

Voids play a major role in our lives. They need to be assessed and addressed. They are not to be feared; they are to be managed. In fact, having voids can be a positive thing. They may force us to concentrate on an energy our soul needs for its well-being or perhaps avoid it so we can be released from its energy to pursue other directions in life. Remember the people we mentioned earlier who had a void[s] in their charts: General George Patton, Princess Diana, Marilyn Monroe, Mother Teresa, Amelia Earhart, Charles Lindberg, Martin Luther King, William Shakespeare, Abraham Lincoln, Albert Einstein, Albert Schweitzer, Charles Darwin and Helen Keller? These were distinguished souls who did great things, so having voids does not preclude us from being of service or exuding a substantive life. Almost every one of us has a void or voids in our name. Why? Only God knows for certain. Our lives are in His hands and we would be wise to surrender to His Wisdom.

This said, it is a fact that voids can create problems, especially if they're located in the Challenge position of the *Life Matrix* which is explained in *The King's Book of Numerology II: Forecasting - Part I*. There is no sense in discussing such things at this time because it would only complicate the matter of basic love and attraction between people. In fact, having voids may well play a positive role in the love match process. Many people who have voids can have beautiful partnerships, especially if their partner's chart contains the ciphers that are void in their chart. When voids are fulfilled, however they're fulfilled, people are fulfilled and potentially happier than they would be otherwise. Therefore, if one person's Loveline or the Loveline Mix contains the numbers that are voided in the other person's Loveline, this is a good thing because the numbers present in the other person or in the Mix will satisfy the voids and the sense of loss that accompany them.

One other issue needs to be mentioned, however. That is in the naming of children. Because voids, especially Grand Voids, are potentially problematic, when naming children it would be of value to make sure the full natal name contained no voids. Having no voids would mitigate any major issues and their subsequent problems should they occur in life. Yet, these things are all in God's hands. A person reading this book may be given such knowledge to help an incoming soul, while people not privy to such information would be acting in concert with the given destiny of their child or children. The best advice is to always trust in God and His Judgment. He knows what is ultimately best for every soul, and He may well want a person to have a void or voids in his or her life to fulfill the script that is destined for that soul.

Chapter Twelve

LOVE NOTES

Let's wrap up. There are just a few simple things we need to do to know our life, loves and relationships in 5 minutes. Of course, beyond this book, one's study can be continued if one wishes. There is much to know about numerology, its truth and wonderful application to our lives. We've just touched on one of its aspects. Further knowledge is available through *The King's Book of Numerology, Volume I: Foundations & Fundamentals*, *The King's Book of Numerology II: Forecasting - Part I*, and other books available at RichardKing.Net.

What to do from here? Start creating *Lovelines*, *Loveline Matches* and *Loveline Mixes*. Start with yourself and then study your loved ones and close friends. This is the best way to learn because we know who we are and we know our family and friends better than anyone. Therefore, we can learn to associate people's numbers with their lives. The more charts we study, the more we learn. After studying the seven *Loveline* components: Lifepath, Expression, Performance, Soul, Material Soul, Nature and Material Nature, construct a chart on yourself, cross-referencing your numbers with the keywords listed in Chapter Seven, *The Loveline*. Follow the basic steps below.

Step 1. *The Extended Loveline* [Chapter Seven]

Simple Letter Value Chart									
The Letters	A	B	C	D	E	F	G	H	I
	J	K	L	M	N	O	P	Q	R
	S	T	U	V	W	X	Y	Z	
Number Value	1	2	3	4	5	6	7	8	9

Using the Simple Letter Value Chart, compute the components of the Loveline. Fill in each of their numbers in the "#" column and list a few keywords to begin focusing on the personality makeup of the person. Study all of the keywords for each number to expand the understanding of its category. Use your intuition too. It's a valuable asset to the logic part of the assessment process. Here is a blank form which can be easily reconstructed on your computer.

Name:_____

	#	Brief List of Keywords
Lifepath		
Expression		
Performance		
Soul		
Material Soul		
Nature		
Material Nature		

Step 2. *The Loveline Match* [Chapter Eight]

After the Lovelines are created, generate the *Loveline Match* between you and the other person. Then simply connect the appropriate components with a line using a pen or pencil. Here are some things to remember:

1. Check for *Soul Release* first.
2. Check for *Expression to Performance*.
    *These are the most important connections of the Internal and External aspects of the Lovelines.
3. Check for *Nature Release*.
4. Check for other *Umbrella* connections.
5. Check for other connections in general.
6. Compute the total number of connections.
7. Note any voids.

Loveline Matrix

_____ & _____

	Person # 1			Person # 2	
External	Lifepath			Lifepath	External
	Expression			Expression	
	P/E			P/E	
Internal	Soul			Soul	Internal
	Material Soul			Material Soul	
	Nature			Nature	
	Material Nature			Material Nature	
	First Name			First Name	
	Connections: Person #1 =				
	Connections: Person #2 =				
	Total Connections: Persons #1 & #2 =				

Step 3. *The Loveline Mix* [Chapter Nine]

The final step is to create the Loveline Mix. As we've seen, the Loveline Match is a powerful tool but the Loveline Mix will give us specific information about the relationship itself, not just the other person. Therefore, it is a critical piece of the relationship puzzle. Once the chart is completed, look for 2s and 7s in the Mix which can be, but not always, problematic. Look for other similarities, numerical correspondences and opposing pairs: 1 & 2; 4 & 5; 7 & 8. Finally, compute the total number of all connections between the Match and the Mix. The more connections the better. Also insure that both people's numbers harmonize with the other person and the Mix. Lovelines favoring only one person don't bode well for an excellent relationship. Both partners must be satisfied to insure fulfillment and happiness. That's it. Develop these simple and easy skills and you're on the way to truly being The 5 Minute L♥ver!

Loveline Mix

_____ & _____

		#1	Mix	#2		
External	Lifepath				Lifepath	External
	Expression				Expression	
	P/E				P/E	
Internal	Soul				Soul	Internal
	Material Soul				Material Soul	
	Nature				Nature	
	Material Nature				Material Nature	
	First Name				First Name	
Total Connections: #1 =						
Total Connections: #2 =						
Total Connections in the Mix =						

Richard Andrew King
~ Books ~
www.richardking.net

The King's Book of Numerology
Volume 1-Foundations & Fundamentals

The King's Book of Numerology, Volume 1-Foundations & Fundamentals provides complete descriptions of Basic Numbers, Double Numbers, Purifier Numbers, Master Numbers, the Letters in Simple and Specific form as well as the Basic Matrix, the numerological blueprint of our lives.

~

"*The King's Book of Numerology* series contains new information that informs and predicts more completely and accurately than any previously published numerological work. It brings back the empowered sciences of long ago, information long since lost upon this plane." ~ G. Shaver

"The best numerology book I've ever read." ~ M.W.

"I've learned as much about numerology from *The King's Book of Numerology* the last few days than I have in my past five years of study." ~ Frank M.

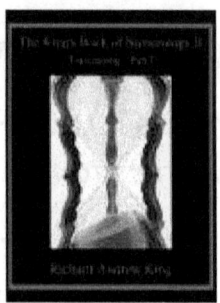

The King's Book of Numerology II
Forecasting - Part 1

The King's Book of Numerology II: Forecasting - Part 1 is dedicated to opening the door to the divine blueprint of our lives. That plan, that divine blueprint of destiny, is exact, precise, unchangeable, unalterable and . . . knowable, at least in general terms. Once this awareness of a predetermined fate becomes established through application of numbers and their truths, our understanding and consciousness of life will, no doubt, change. We will begin to see ourselves as part of an immense spiritual super-structure far beyond our current ability to comprehend, understand or perceive. Life will take on new meaning and, perhaps, we will even begin to awaken to greater spiritual truths. Subjects covered: Life Cycle Patterns, The Pinnacle/Challenge Matrix, Epoch Timeline, Voids, Case Studies and much more.

Blueprint of a Princess
Diana Frances Spencer - Queen of Hearts

The tragic death of Princess Diana of Wales - the most famous, the most photographed, the most written about woman of the modern world and possibly of all time - was one of the most shocking and saddening events of the late Twentieth Century. Not since the assassination of American President John Fitzgerald Kennedy in 1963, has such an event captured the attention of the world. On that ill-fated Sunday of 31 August 1997, and the following week until her funeral, there was much discussion and reflection of the Queen of Hearts, the People's Princess, England's Rose. But in all of the media news coverage, there was no discussion given to the cosmic aspects of her life and death. This book is dedicated to addressing those issues through The King's Numerology. Its purpose and hope is to offer some consolation and explanation as to that one question so poignantly written on a card of condolence left with the multitude of flowers before the gates of Buckingham Palace. . . "Why?"

~

"After learning from King's numerological teaching, it is impossible to conceive of going back to that 'twilight naive and foggy' state of being where one can only guess or hint at the truths, motivations and directions of one's life that is Pre-King. Not only do I recommend this book, but I suggest it and his other numerology books as absolutely necessary for the library of anyone even remotely interested in the science of numerology." ~ Hunter Stowers

Messages from the Masters
Timeless Truths for Spiritual Seekers

In a time where there is more need for enlightenment than ever before, *Messages from the Masters: Timeless Truths for Spiritual Seekers* offers timeless truths for genuine seekers thirsty for spiritual nectar.

Masters are the Ph.D.s of the universe, the Light Bearers of the Divine Flame. Their knowledge and wisdom are supreme. They have no equal. Although appearing human, they are not. Masters are the exalted Sons of God. Their chief duty is to rescue souls, liberating them from the maniacal maelstrom and madness of the material world and returning them to their eternal Home with the Lord.

Messages from the Masters is a rich source of hundreds of quotes from a cavalcade of nine Perfect Saints throughout the last six hundred years: Guru Ravidas, Kabir, Guru Nanak, Tulsi Sahib, Swami Ji Maharaj, Baba Jaimal Singh, Sawan Singh, Jagat Singh and Charan Singh. The messages in this book focus on the importance of the Divine Diet, the priceless Human Form, Reincarnation, the World, the Negative Power and Soul Food.

Warning! *Messages from the Masters* is not for the faint of heart or the worldly-minded. Masters come into the world to sever our attachment to it, not make it a paradise. Although the epitome of love and wisdom, they shoot straight from the hip, pull no punches, favor no religion. Their universal message of soul liberation is reflected in the statement of Saint Maharaj Charan Singh: *Just live in the creation and get out of it*!

99 Poems of the Spirit

99 Poems of the Spirit draws from the writings of Perfect Saints, Masters, Mystics and Sacred Scriptures. Designed to lift the consciousness, mind and heart, all of the poems are original works by Richard King. Their purpose is to help connect the reader with the mystic side of life in order to enhance the process of self-realization while advancing on the spiritual path and climbing the ladder leading to the ultimate attainment of God Realization. It is a treasure chest of poetic spiritual gems offered to excite, educate and stimulate the mind and soul in the glorious journey of spiritual ascent.

A few selected poem titles are:

A Thousand Mile Journey
Animal Food
Awake, Dear Soul
Between Two Worlds
Cards of Life
Child of the Light
City of the Dead
Glittering Lights
Karma
King of Fools
Lady of the Light
Reaping Weeping
Serious Business
The Wheel
We Reap the Deeds
World of Fools

The Age of the Female
A Thousand Years of Yin

The Age of the Female: A Thousand Years of Yin highlights the profound and extraordinary ascent of the female in the modern world, placing her center stage in the global spotlight as presidents and leaders of nations, titans of industry, corporate executives, military generals, media magnets, doctors, lawyers and a whole host of other prestigious titles normally associated with the male. Why has her rise to prominence been so rapid, especially in consideration of historic time? Why also has there been an increased interest in other people's lives in our society, in competitive athletics, personal data collection and the exploration of space and other worlds? *The Age of the Female: A Thousand Years of Yin* answers these questions. It is an insightful and exciting read into these mysteries, offering compelling and irrefutable evidence through the ancient science and art of numerology that, indeed, the age of the female has arrived and the next thousand years belong, not to him, but to her.

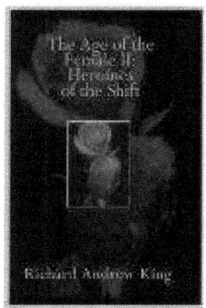

The Age of the Female II
Heroines of the Shift

The Age of the Female II: Heroines of the Shift continues the remarkable journey of the female's ascent in the modern world of the 2nd Millennium. This installment is a general read in five chapters honoring the accomplishments of women in categories of female firsts, female Nobel laureates, female athletes, female icons and female quotations. The achievements of the women featured in *The Age of the Female II: Heroines of the Shift* are deserving of respect and admiration. Their lives, challenges and successes are motivational catalysts for every individual to be the best he or she can be and to honor the very essence of what it is to be human. *The Age of the Female II: Heroines of the Shift* is intended to be an inspiring and educational read for everyone, not just women but men, too, offering knowledge and insight of the depth, power and daring-do of women as their Yin energy rises upon the global stage in this millennium which destiny has irrefutably marked as the Age of the Female.

The Black Belt Book of Life
Secrets of a Martial Arts Master

The mystery and mystique of the martial arts is not only ages old, it's legend. Revered throughout the world, martial arts is a treasure chest of life secrets that transcend the boundaries of combat to include the expanse of life and living. Arguably, it is the greatest developmental system on earth for teaching the integration of body, mind and spirit.

The Black Belt Book of Life: Secrets of a Martial Arts Master is not about physical fighting strategies and tactics. It is about concepts and principles we learn though martial arts training that can help us in the struggle of life, in the journey to conquer ourselves and gain the golden ring of our own completeness because in the end a true Black Belt should be a realized soul who, having engaged the enemy - himself - finds himself at the end of the journey, triumphant.

The Black Belt Book of Life: Secrets of a Martial Arts Master reveals many secrets of martial arts training, sharing these truths in quick and easy to read vignettes to benefit martial artists and the general public as well. It is a book for all readers, not just martial artists, both males and females, especially the youth of today who are in search of a foundation to guide their lives.

To order books, go to

www.RichardKing.Net

Contact

Richard Andrew King

PO Box 3621

Laguna Hills, CA 92654

www.RichardKing.Net

www.YourLoveNumbers.com

Email: rich@richardking.net

Email: arichking@att.net

www.ingramcontent.com/pod-product-compliance
Lightning Source LLC
Chambersburg PA
CBHW071420150426
43191CB00008B/980